The printed endpapers of this edition feature two medieval
motifs – the rose and the estoile – larger versions of which
were discovered in 1999 under obscuring paintwork on the walls of
the Parvis Room in St Laurence's church.
They have been recreated in part
in the Parvis Room by Peter and Deborah Klein who also kindly
supplied the artwork for these endpapers.

THE CONCISE HISTORY OF LUDLOW

A place of fame and antiquity

William Stukeley, c.1722

David Lloyd MBE

MERLIN UNWIN BOOKS
Ludlow

Published for the Ludlow Historical Research Group with the generous assistance
of a Millenium Festival Award

Half the author's royalties will be divided among the following:
The Fabric Trust for St Laurence, Ludlow, The Friends of Whitcliffe and The Weirs Trust

Published by:
Merlin Unwin Books
Palmers House
7 Corve Street, Ludlow
Shropshire SY8 1DB. U.K.
Tel: 01584 877456
Fax: 01584 877457
Email: books@merlinunwin.co.uk
Web: www.merlinunwin.co.uk

Hardback ISBN 1 873674 41 4
Paperback ISBN 1 873674 42 2
British Library Catalogueing-in-Publication Data:
A catalogue record of this book is available from the British Library.

Edited and published by Merlin Unwin Books, Ludlow.
Designed by Mary Hayter, Hamlyn Design, Ludlow.
Printed and bound in Great Britain by Biddles Ltd, Guildford.

CONTENTS

Inset: (above: O.S. 10,560 (1939); shows the historic town, railway line and suburbs to east and north.
Map: O.S.1: 2,500 (1885); shows the streets, burgages and principal buildings of the town centre, prior to the development of the 20th century.

Preface and Acknowledgments

The idea for this book came from the late Peter Bell. As a bookseller he saw the need for a single-volume History of Ludlow which was authoritative, yet affordable. Such a book, he said, was often asked for: by Ludlow residents, by visitors, by students needing a basis for more detailed study. The Concise History of Ludlow seeks to meet this need.

Peter's premature death in 1997 was a great loss to Ludlow. The book is dedicated to his memory, not only because of the demand which he identified but also for the encouragement which he, for many years Ludlow's leading bookseller, gave to publications in local history.

The book draws on the scholarly researches of many people, most of them associated with the Ludlow Historical Research Group since its formation in 1976. A particular debt is due to my old school friend Michael Faraday, whose meticulous transcriptions of medieval and early modern documents, many of them at the Public Record Office in London, have provided information rarely available to provincial local historians. His own Ludlow, 1085-1660: A Social, Economic and Political History (1991) is a treasure house of knowledge and perception, on which I have often drawn. Other scholarly contributions, often from unpublished work, have come from Peter Klein, Dr Martin Speight, Christopher Train CB, and Dr Derrick Williams OBE. Madge Moran FSA has inspired and directed the recording, interpretation and dating of Ludlow buildings, while the late Stephen Dornan had a great influence on my understanding of eighteenth century Ludlow. I am grateful to the many local people, often from long-established Ludlow families, who have lent or given me pictures of the town, and to all those who have attended the classes and day schools on Ludlow with which I have been involved. Over many years I have received a great deal of help and co-operation from the staff of record offices and libraries, especially at Birmingham, Hereford and Shrewsbury; and from staff at Ludlow Museum, especially John Norton MBE, and Kate Andrew.

It was decided at the outset not to include footnotes in this publication; but complete sets of references, and precise acknowledgments of the information supplied by others, have been lodged at Ludlow Library, Shropshire Centre for Records and Research, and Hereford County Record Office, where they can be consulted by scholars.

I am grateful to the following for reading the draft text: Dr Peter Borsay, University of Wales; Revd Dr Brian Curnew, Rector of Ludlow; Michael Faraday;

Peter Klein; Madge Moran FSA; Dr Martin Speight; Sir Keith Thomas, President of Corpus Christi College, Oxford; and Dr Barrie Trinder. They have all made constructive comments and suggestions which have greatly enhanced this book. Final responsibility for the text, however, is entirely my own. I am especially grateful to Keith Thomas, who spends some of his time in Ludlow, for writing the foreword.

Thanks are due to The Ludlow Association for the Millennium Celebrations, especially its Chairman, Alan Poulton, for promoting this publication as a millennium project. The publishers, Merlin and Karen Unwin, national leaders in their specialist field of angling, agreed with alacrity to publish this book. It has been a joy to work with them and I hope they will not regret their foray into local history. We agreed that local talent should be used where possible, and the book has been enriched by Mary Hayter's design skills and by John McColgan's maps. The cover design incorporates photographs by Gareth Thomas and Merlin Unwin.

Illustrations on the pages numbered below and permission to reproduce them have kindly been given by: Robert Auld 76; Peter Bartlett 43, 62; Offentliche Kunstsammlung, Basel, Switzerland 121; Birmingham University Archaeological Unit 58; Bodleian Library 45, 48, 50, 74, 82; British Library 20, 45, 97; Country Life 129; Rector and Churchwardens of St Giles Parish Church, Ludford 93; Ivan Hall 90/91, 140; Hereford Public Library 138; Rose Hern 157; Graham Wilson Lloyd 31; Ludlow Town Council 62, 84; John Lush 34, 47, 55; McCartneys 151; Madge Moran 53; John McGolgan and Mary Hayter 4, 11, 15, 17, 25, 26, 71, 72/73, 101, 111, 122, 136, 149; National Portrait Gallery 63; Robin Newman 134; John Morton MBE 61; Judith Parish 108; Plymouth Estates 22; Rector and Churchwardens of St Laurence's Parish Church 70, 83; Celia Rowlands 147; Royal British Legion 157; Humphrey Salwey 9; Noel Shepherdson 54; Shropshire County Museum Service 79; Shropshire Magazine 123, 138; Shropshire Records and Research 32, 118, 138; Joy Wheeler-Phillips 82.

FOREWORD

Visitors to Ludlow quickly realise that they have come to a place of exceptional historical interest. Wherever one looks, one sees striking survivals of the past: the superbly-situated castle, the twelfth-century street-plan, the magnificent perpendicular church, the timber-framed buildings and the handsome Georgian town houses. All are reminders that what is now a peaceful market town was once a seat of royal government and a social centre of some pretensions. It was here that Henry VIII's son, Prince Arthur, came in 1501 with his bride, Catherine of Aragon, and here that he died a few months later; and it was here that Milton's masque Comus was first performed in 1634. At the end of the nineteenth century it was Ludlow which provided the focus for the poignant longings of A. E. Housman's The Shropshire Lad.

The town has been fortunate in its historians. In the nineteenth century the two Thomas Wrights, father and son, told the story of Ludlow and its buildings with great antiquarian learning. In the early twentieth century Sir William St John Hope did important work on the history of the castle and on Ludlow as a 'planned town.' More recently Michael Faraday has produced an excellent history of Ludlow 1085-1660 (1991), while Peter Borsay has illuminated Ludlow's history as a social centre in his The English Urban Renaissance (1989).

David Lloyd belongs in this fine tradition. During the past twenty years or so, his active role in the Ludlow Historical Research Group has resulted in many valuable publications about the town and its buildings. Now he brings together the work of previous scholars, combined with the fruits of his own archival and archaeological research, to produce the first history of Ludlow to run from its geological origins to the end of the twentieth century. He is an author who knows the town intimately and loves what he knows. He has produced an indispensable guide to Ludlow's past which no-one, whether visitor or resident, should be without.

Keith Thomas   The Broad Gate
Corpus Christi College   Ludlow
Oxford

In memory of Peter Bell
(1945-97) bookseller

CHAPTER ONE

These words were written in 1943 by the poet John Betjeman, a connoisseur of English towns and townscapes. They are but one of a long line of eulogistic comments on Ludlow, spanning eight centuries. In 1188 Giraldus Cambrensis, touring Wales and the Marches to recruit supporters for King Richard's crusade to the Holy Land, observed 'the noble castle of Ludlow' as he passed along what is now Burway Lane. In 1587 the Shrewsbury poet Thomas Churchyard, caught the essence of Ludlow's urban charm when he wrote in The Worthiness of Wales

> The towne doth stand most part upon an hill,
> Built well and fayre, with streates both large and wide ...
> And who that lists to walke the towne about,
> Shall find therein some rare and pleasant things ...

In 1795 another traveller round Wales, Henry Skrine of Worle in Somerset, expressed surprise that 'nature and art have combined to create so polished a town in a remote corner of the kingdom', while in Country Life in 1943 Christopher Hussey declared that 'the whole place is a national monument'.

This fine panoramic view of Ludlow, painted in 1722, shows the hill-top site of the town, with the River Teme forming a wide crescent to the west and south. Though many houses had been rebuilt, the general appearance of the town in 1722 was little changed from what it had been in Churchyard's time.

Ludlow is situated in the south of Shropshire, a few miles east of the Welsh border. It occupies a central position on the Welsh Marches, the historic frontier zone between England and Wales, and lies half way between Chester in the north and Chepstow in the south. Most of the place names in the vicinity of Ludlow, such as Caynham and Steventon, are Anglo-Saxon, but names of Welsh origin, such as Walcot, occur only a few miles away. In the 16th and 17th centuries Ludlow was the administrative capital of Wales, while the Welsh gentry were prominent among those who had houses in the town in the eighteenth century. People of Welsh origin have always played a part in the life of the town, pre-eminent among them the various branches of the Herberts whose common ancestor came from Monmouthshire.

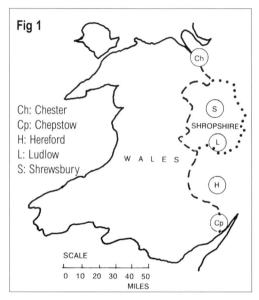

Fig 1

Ch: Chester
Cp: Chepstow
H: Hereford
L: Ludlow
S: Shrewsbury

SCALE

0 10 20 30 40 50
MILES

The town lies near the southern edge of a varied topographical area of great beauty often called 'the south Shropshire uplands'. The highest land is that of the Clee Hills, where Titterstone Clee and the two peaks of the Brown Clee - Abdon Burf and Clee Burf - rise high above the surrounding valleys, drained by the Teme and its tributaries. To the north and west the Brown Clee is bordered by Corvedale, the wide valley of the Corve, from which the land rises to the north west to Wenlock Edge and the adjoining hills. These hills, breached by the River Onny between Stokesay and Onibury, swing round to the west and south west of Ludlow, where they are known as Bringewood Chase and High Vinnals. The poet A.E. Housman reflects the mood of this hill-and-vale countryside with lines such as:

> Wenlock Edge was umbered
> And bright was Abdon Burf
> And warm between them slumbered
> The smooth green miles of turf

There are glimpses of the surrounding hills from most parts of central Ludlow, while the names of suburban roads such as Greenacres and Bringewood View remind us that beautiful countryside is never far away. It is understandable, therefore, that the journalist Christopher Wordsworth, writing in Village England in 1981, described Ludlow as 'a crown on green velvet'.

CHAPTER TWO

THE SITE OF LUDLOW AND ITS PRE-URBAN DEVELOPMENT

Geology

The topographical variety of the Ludlow district reflects local geology, with many different types of rock outcropping in a small area. This is a classic region for the study of geology, especially of the rocks of the Silurian series, which were first classified here by Sir Roderick Murchison in the 1830s, incorporating the work of local amateurs. Fig. 2 shows a simplified geological map of the area with the older marine Silurian rocks to the west and the younger Old Red Sandstone and Carboniferous strata to the east.

The Silurian rocks were laid down in tropical seas more than 400 million years ago. At times fine mud was deposited in deep water, which has hardened into shales and mudstones. When the sea was shallower, corals and other lime-producing creatures thrived, forming limestones. These rocks were later folded into a tapering arch or anticline, the softer shales being eroded to form valleys, while the resistant limestones were left upstanding as escarpments. The steep 'white' slopes of calcareous siltstones and shelly limestones which give Whitcliffe its name are just one local exposure. This Whitcliffe rock, yielding a 'chunky' limestone, has provided the town's chief building stone, but sadly it is prone to weathering.

FIG 2
A simplified geological map of the Ludlow area

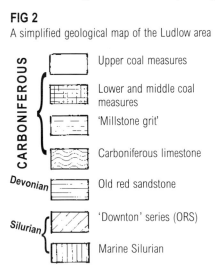

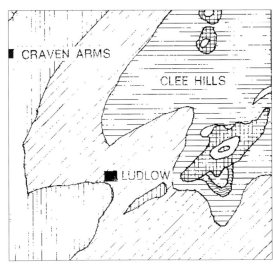

Another notable outcrop is that of the Ludlow Bone Bed at Ludford Corner. This is a thin gingerbread-like layer of dark sand, with numerous fragmentary remains of some of the earliest fish. It marks the transition from marine Silurian rocks to the younger Downtonian series.

The Downtonian strata around Ludlow consist partly of red marls, which form the undulating land north and east of the town. Those closest to Ludlow have been fired for bricks since the 17th century or earlier, and run through to Fishmore Road, where a brickworks closed as recently as 1948. Further east are the Old Red Sandstone rocks, which form a plateau at the base of the Clee Hills. These were laid down in semi-arid continental conditions between 400 and 350 million years ago. They were succeeded by the younger Carboniferous rocks which survive as the upper parts of the Clee Hills and where some coal measures occur, the legacy of the great deltas with tropical vegetation which once covered this area. The coal measures were mined from the Middle Ages, providing Ludlow with an important source of fuel, while the ironstones which also occurred were the basis of a rural iron industry, using local charcoal. These rocks owed their preservation to capping by dolerite, a basaltic igneous rock known as dhustone, which is still quarried for road metal. The resulting 'high reared head of Clee' is a familiar part of the skyline.

The rocks were subjected to folding and other pressures, ripples of great earth movements in Europe and further afield. They were then eroded by rivers and other processes, culminating in the great Ice Age which began about two million years ago. The ice advanced and retreated four times, the effects on the Ludlow district probably being greatest in the later periods, when torrents of melt water cut

An exposure of the Ludlow Bone Bed on the north side of the Wigmore Road. The outcrop, marked by the shadowed line, has been eroded by geologists.

overflow channels through the previous watersheds, causing rivers to be diverted from earlier courses. Downton Gorge was formed in this way and so too was the steep-sided valley of the Teme between Whitcliffe and the town of Ludlow.

This early nineteenth century print, though some details are slightly romanticised, shows how the valley of the River Teme narrows as the river enters the steep-sided gorge at Ludlow.

The steep slopes beneath the castle and the cliffs of Whitcliffe opposite are the result of these dramatic events. Equally important for the town's development were the natural rapids along this stretch of the river, especially between Lower Mill Street and the bottom of Holdgate Fee, where the river has a gradient of 1:16. These rapids caused 'the loud waters' which gave the prefix 'lud' to the place name Ludlow, but they are less apparent now than formerly because of the weirs built to provide the head of water needed to drive the town's numerous mills.

Another legacy of the Ice Age are the gravel and alluvial terraces which are a feature of the Teme valley. The higher gravels, which give their name to Gravel Hill and which contained the sand which gave its name to Sandpits as early as the 14th century, were deposited when the river was at a higher level than at present. The gravels of a later valley floor are even more extensive, forming an impressive river terrace south-east of Bromfield, part of which, known as 'the Old Field' - now the Racecourse – attracted a large Bronze Age settlement.

Relief

The historic core of Ludlow occupies the top and sides of a tilted block of land projecting westwards from higher ground to the east, the latter now being occupied by Victorian and later suburbs. The top of the block provides a broad, almost level ridge, at a height of about 120 metres. The castle, the parish church and the original market place are on this ridge, which provided an ideal level site for building and trading. To the south, the land drops to the River Teme, a distance of about a third of a mile, with a gradient of 1:16. Many of the houses of the medieval town were on this slope, with the streets climbing steadily from the river to the market place. To the north, where the slope reflects a geological fault, the gradient in places is 1:6, though in Linney it then drops almost imperceptibly to reach the River Corve. Corve Street, the principal routeway out of town to the north, takes a rather gentler slope, although there is a gradient of 1:12 as it drops down from the Bull Ring. Corve Street is the longest of the town's main residential streets, stretching half a mile to the Corve Bridge.

This view of the town centre, photographed in the 1970s, shows the historic market place, the parish church and adjoining buildings on the wide ridge running eastwards from the castle. It also shows some of the houses of Sandpits Avenue and other suburbs on higher land rising towards the slopes of Titterstone Clee Hill in the far distance.

14

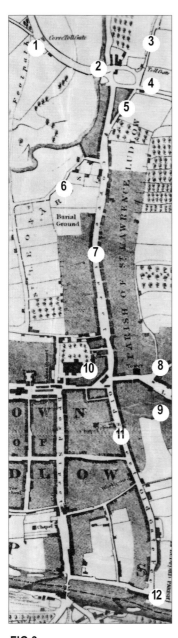

FIG.3
This section of a map of Ludlow
made in 1832 is used to show
selected features of the
pre-urban landscape.

Pre-urban development

Although there is no firm evidence of settlement on
the site of Ludlow until the late eleventh
century, the earlier activities of man in the area created a framework for urban development. Existing
trackways, in particular, were a major influence. The
most important of these was the pre-historic north-south
routeway now followed by the line of Corve Street and
Old Street - the latter street name itself a hint of ancient
origins. The route was certainly used in Roman times,
probably crossing the River Teme at the bottom of Old
Street. Excavations in the early 1960's revealed evidence
of Roman engineering, namely 'a thickness of two to
three feet of dirty compact hardcore' which lay 'on a firm
mass of broken shale'. The road probably crossed the
River Corve at or near Corve Bridge and then continued north westwards towards Bromfield. At Corve
Bridge this track intersected with the allegedly older
'Clun-Clee ridgeway'. This came from Bromfield along
the line of Burway Lane and followed the present New
Road towards the Severn Valley. Microliths from the
Mesolithic period (8,000 - 4,500 BC) have been found
along the ridgeway, but it seems to have been most used
in the more recent Neolithic and Beaker periods, when
artefacts found include several close to Ludlow, such as an
axe in Oakly Park, Bromfield. Map analysis suggests that
another ancient track came along Fishmore Road and St
Mary's Lane and then by the part of Linney which now
runs beside St Leonard's churchyard. The triangle
between St Mary's Lane, Lower Corve Street and the
western end of New Road, though colonised by buildings in the Middle Ages, is an enduring town-plan relic
of this ancient road inter-change.

1	Burway Lane	5 St Mary's Lane	11 Old Street
2	Early crossing place of the River Corve	6 Part of Linney	12 Site of ford across the River Teme
		7 Corve Street	
3	Fishmore Road	8 Upper Galdeford	
4	New Road	9 Lower Galdeford	
		10 Site of tumulus	

Another element in the pre-urban landscape was the tumulus or burial mound which is reputed to have stood on part of the site of the later parish church. The tradition that this tumulus was removed when the church was rebuilt and enlarged in 1199 is confirmed in the Llandaff Chronicle, compiled about 1338. This tumulus can be associated with the Bronze Age settlement on the Old Field at Bromfield. With some 20 barrows and other features scattered over the level gravel terrace, this is a prehistoric site of great importance - and it is reasonable to suppose that some burials, perhaps those of special significance, took place at Ludlow, on the crest of the ridge which closes the view south from Bromfield. The ridge may have served as a boundary, a common location for tumuli. The tumulus was certainly a prominent enough feature to provide the suffix hlaw or low in the place name Ludlow; 'low' being Anglo-Saxon for tumulus - and it may well have been a focus for trackways which later became Lower and Upper Galdeford.

Anglo-Saxon settlement probably reached south Shropshire in the early seventh century, when the area was part of the kingdom of the Magonsaete, later the diocese of Hereford. It is likely that the earliest Anglo-Saxon settlements are those with 'ham' endings such as Caynham and Corfham, and it is sometimes claimed that the part of Ludlow now called Dinham is such a place-name, indicating a pre-Norman Conquest settlement. But recent work challenges this view, for the earliest known form is 'Dynan', which is a French name perhaps derived from Joce de Dinan, who had possession of Ludlow in the 1140's and who came from Brittany. Linney, however, which refers to the steep slope north of the town centre and to the low-lying land beyond, is certainly an Anglo-Saxon place name, probably referring to 'the dry land' above the flax-producing area from which linen was produced. This may have been wild flax, easily gathered from the routeway a short distance away - and an important indicator of the early economic usefulness of this area.

This well preserved barrow at Round Hill near Pennerley, 15 miles north west of Ludlow, is perhaps the kind of 'low' which was once at Ludlow.

This steep slope, now called Upper Linney, was the dry land overlooking the alluvial plain of the River Teme where flax once grew.

CHAPTER THREE

THE NORMAN CASTLE AND PLANNED TOWN

The Ludlow area in 1086

The Domesday Book survey of 1086 gives a glimpse of the late Anglo-Saxon landscape and settlement pattern, as conquered by the Normans following the invasion of 1066. Two of the most populated parishes in south Shropshire were Bromfield and Stanton, later called Stanton Lacy, while to the south, partly across the River Teme in Herefordshire, was the smaller parish of Ludford, which included the manor of Steventon. The ancient parish boundary between Stanton Lacy and Ludford is still a prominent feature at Rock Lane, with a continuation in Friars' Walk.

The modern town of Ludlow covers parts of all three parishes, but almost all the historic town was part of Stanton. Ludlow and Stanton shared a common seigneurial history in the post-Norman period, when they belonged to the powerful Lacy family. Until the 19th century part of Linney remained an outlying portion of Stanton Lacy, suggesting strongly that the planned town had been carved from the rural manor. Many new towns were created by the Normans in this way out of existing large manors. Other Shropshire examples are Bridgnorth from the manor of Morville and Bishops Castle from Lydbury North. The south-eastern part of Ludlow, however, seems to have come out of Ludford, and has a different seigneurial history: the area adjoining lower Old Street was long known as Holdgate Fee, because of dues paid to the Lord of Holdgate in Corvedale. The modern names Lower and Upper Fee reflect this early pattern of land-holding.

FIG. 4
Parish boundaries before 1884

A   Detached part of Stanton Lacy
B   Rock Lane
C   Part of Friars' Walk
D   Detached part of Ludford
E   Holdgate Fee

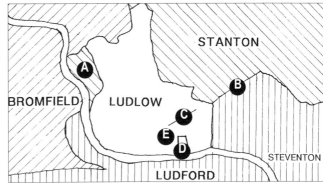

The Lacys

Ludlow is one of a large group of new towns which were initiated by a lay lord or seigneur, rather than by the King, a religious house or a bishop. For most of the period before 1241 the parent manor of Stanton and the new town of Ludlow were among the estates of the Lacy family, who came from Lassy in Normandy. Lassy lies south west of Falaise, where William Duke of Normandy had his own great castle, and where a list of the knights who followed him across the English Channel in 1066 is now displayed in the Town Hall. One of these knights was Walter Lacy I. He was one of a group of Marcher lords who were given an unusually large number of manors in return for undertaking the onerous duty of guarding the English frontier against the still unconquered Welsh. The Lacys held over 200 manors, many of them in Herefordshire, where a number were administered together as the Honour of Weobley, which became another Norman new town. Stanton emerged as the caput (head) of a distinct group of manors further to the north, and Ludlow was eventually the largest Lacy stronghold in the Marches.

The Lacys were strong personalities, some of whom often quarrelled with their king. Roger I was banished for rebellion in 1096, while in the time of Walter II Ludlow Castle was sometimes taken into royal custody. Hugh II and Walter II spent much of their time in Ireland, where Hugh II was Justicar from 1177 to 1184. Another strong personality was Payn fitz John, son-in-law to Hugh I, who was Sheriff of Shropshire during the 1130s. An opponent of the Lacys was Joce de Dinan, a Breton who held Ludlow Castle during part of the confused reign of Stephen, 1135-54. He features in The Fitzwarine Romance, an early 14th century tale based on an earlier poem which portrays him as building a bridge over the River Teme.

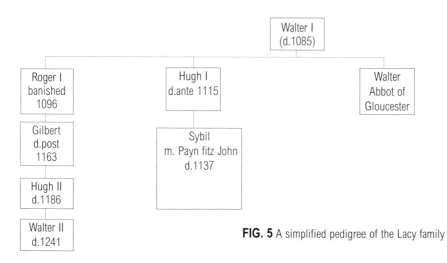

FIG. 5 A simplified pedigree of the Lacy family

18

Ludlow Castle

The castle was almost certainly the earliest contribution by the Normans to Ludlow's town plan. It is not mentioned in the Domesday Book of 1086, though this does not necessarily preclude an earlier date. Roger Lacy I, who succeeded to his father's estates in 1085, was later credited with building the first castle, in which case the work must have started before his banishment in 1095. The architectural evidence is consistent with such a date, especially the capitals in the basement of the great tower, which are of a very crude design. There is force indeed in the suggestion that the castle may have been started in or just before 1088, the year when Roger first rebelled against William II. He would have needed a castle in the kind of well-defended position provided by the virgin site in the corner of his large manor of Stanton.

The elliptical shape of the inner bailey, with its early flanking towers and gatehouse/keep, and also the round nave of the chapel of St Mary Magdalene, can be seen on this postcard of the 1920s.

The oldest part of the castle is the inner bailey, where the curtain wall, which is between five and six feet thick, has an elliptical shape. To the north and west, above the steep slopes of the Teme Gorge, there are protruding flanking towers, from which archers could cover the intervening walls; while to the south and east, where the level ridge-top provided easy access, the castle was defended by a dry ditch. The original entrance was through a gatehouse which was later raised into a keep or 'great tower'. The gatehouse contained a long passage which was the grand entrance into the castle and was flanked first by doors and then by blind arcading. Later, perhaps about 1130, when Payn fitz John was lord, this gatehouse was 'carried up as a tower' to accommodate a living hall and other rooms. Another surviving Norman building is the Chapel of St Mary Magdalene, which has a round nave. Naves of this kind can often be attributed to the Knights Templars, who arrived in England in 1128, but at Ludlow the dating evidence is ambiguous. Some archaeologists now favour a mid-12th century date, in which case the founder may have been Gilbert Lacy, who repossessed the Lacy estates after 1154 and who is the only Lacy known to have been a Templar.

The castle saw its first recorded action in 1138, during the civil war between Stephen and Matilda, when it was taken from the Lacys by Gervase Pagnal, one of the rebel barons who supported Matilda. A year later it was besieged by an army led by the King himself. Two siege engines were used and the King's personal bravery in rescuing a young ally from a grappling iron was noted by a number of contemporary chroniclers. Later the castle was held by Joce de Dinan, whose young squire was Foulke Fitzwarine, hero of the Fitzwarine Romance.

The ornate west doorway of the round nave of the Norman chapel of St Mary Magdalene, with a glimpse of the blank arcading and the chancel arch.
Drawn in 1822 by the architectural artist John Buckler.

The planting of the new town of Ludlow and its early growth

The foundation of Ludlow was part of the 'unprecedented boom in urban growth' which occurred in the 12th and early 13th centuries. It is estimated that during this period between 400 and 500 new towns were established, and that an even greater number of villages were 'promoted' to urban status. At a time when the population was rapidly increasing, these towns helped to absorb people from the countryside. They also provided venues for quickening economic activity, especially in commerce and manufacturing. In frontier zones such as the Welsh Marches, the towns helped to pacify the surrounding area by establishing marketing links; and some of them, such as Ludlow, provided services for an adjoining castle.

However propitious the times, new towns needed an instigator. Ludlow was one of many towns founded and promoted by its seigneurial lords - the Lacys and their relatives. At first, their motives may have been strategic, for Ludllow castle quickly became a principal Lacy stronghold. But Ludlow was also an investment which yielded income from market tolls, from court fines and from rents which the burgesses paid for their burgages – the plots which they held under the castle lords.

The earliest known references to Ludlow relate to 1138 and 1139. Henry of Huntingdon, who died in 1155, describes the attacks on the castle in those years, referring to it as Ludlow Castle. The use of the place name is an indication of a new settlement, already a distinct entity from the parent parish of Stanton, and suggests strongly that a new town had been laid out. A later chronicle, that of Melsa Abbey in east Yorkshire, adds that at Ludlow and in other places the town as well as the castle was captured in 1139, but as this source did not take on its final form until the 14th century, its reliability is uncertain.

Apart from enigmatic references to a bridge across the River Teme in The Fitzwarine Romance, there are no more references to Ludlow until 1169. These were momentous years, nationally and locally, but records are sparse and documentary silence does not imply lack of activity. Between 1169 and 1199, however, there are 34 references to fines, trading practices and disputes over coinage, all indicating a busy and perhaps thriving community. In the 1180s there is mention of Herbert the Reeve, a sign of some measure of local government. The inclusion of seven burgesses surnamed Ludlow in the Dublin Roll of Burgesses in the late 12th century implies that Ludlow men had followed Hugh Lacy II to Ireland - and that they had been rewarded with grants of property in Dublin.

There are other indications of Ludlow's growth. Before his death in 1186, Hugh Lacy II gave 12 burgages and other land at Ludlow to the Knights Hospitallers of Dinmore, which they used for their chapel of St Leonard. The chapel and burgages were on the west side of the lower part of Corve Street, showing that this part of the town had been laid out before that date. As lower Corve Street is half a mile from the castle, a town of some size was clearly in existence. This is confirmed by the 1189-90 Shropshire returns of the tallage, a tax exacted by the Crown. £7 18s 4d was levied in Ludlow, about a third of that on Shrewsbury, but more than the £5 on Bridgnorth, and a much greater amount than the 33s 4d on the parent manor of Stanton. There are indications that the town expanded further at the end of the century. In 1199, the parish church was rebuilt and enlarged, necessitating the removal of the Bronze Age barrow. The new church was a large one, with a floor area four-fifths that of the present building, and presumably was built to accommodate an increasing population. A dispute about tithes, heard in 1200, shows that the town then had two schools, one of them a grammar school. In the early 13th century the Hospital of St John the Baptist was founded by a Ludlow merchant, and endowed with a fulling mill. The location of the hospital and mill, close to Ludford Bridge and at the bottom of Broad Street, implies that this part of the medieval townscape was already in existence. The small Norman chapel in Dinham, dedicated to St Thomas of Canterbury, was probably consecrated within a generation of his martyrdom in 1172 and suggests that Dinham also had already been laid out.

Details of late 12th century Ludlow buildings: Above: The interior roof ribs of St Thomas's chapel in Dinham. Top right: a flat Norman buttress and moulded plinth on the south wall of St Laurence's.

Below right: Round-headed windows and triangular gable at St Leonard's Chapel, Corve Street, seen on an 18th century sketch.

Early burgesses and their burgages

In the Middle Ages, towns were seen as places of privilege, where the citizens - known as burgesses or freemen - enjoyed many rights. The most important was freedom from the feudal laws of the rural manors, which gave rise to the expression 'Town air breathes free'. One privilege of townsmen was the right to own land, the holding of a burgess being known as a burgage. Burgesses held land 'in burgage tenure', which was a virtual freehold, except for the payment of an annual burgage rent to the lord of the town. Ludlow was one of several towns subject to the 'laws of Breteuil', the Normandy town of William Fitz Osbern, whose services in 1066 were rewarded by lands on the Welsh border, including Hereford. One of the laws of Breteuil was the payment of 12d as an annual burgage rent, a practice which persisted at Ludlow until the late 17th century.

Nothing is known about the first Ludlow burgesses but surnames such as Bitterley, Bromfield, Leinthalle, Lingen and Orleton are common in 13th and 14th century lists of Ludlow residents - and suggest that their ancestors came from the places which bear these names, all of them within ten miles of Ludlow. We have to speculate, however, on the circumstances which allowed migrants to leave the feudal embrace of the rural manors, and on the skills which induced their acceptance as Ludlow burgesses.

Research on later and better-documented new towns, such as Edward I's foundation at Winchelsea, with analysis of the present town plan, gives some insights into the laying out of the Ludlow burgages. At Ludlow, as in many other towns, the perch or pole - 16 and a half feet - was the standard unit of measurement used. In spite of subsequent changes, many Ludlow properties still have widths and lengths which are multiples of that unit. In some parts of the town, standardised burgage dimensions can be detected, as on the east side of Corve Street, where properties were two perches wide and 18 perches deep. One such property was sold as an entity for a railway access road in the 1840s and, as Station Drive, survives as a fossilised burgage plot which exactly conforms to these proportions. Elsewhere, however, burgage widths vary, as on the north side of what is now Church Street, where a two perch plot, now the Valentine Dawes Gallery, is between plots which are three perches wide: Hosier's Almshouses to the east, the Rose and Crown with its street frontage shops to the west.

Stages in the growth of Ludlow, as suggested by plan analysis

The documentary sources cited above are sufficient to show the establishment of a town at Ludlow by 1138 or earlier - and indicate its growing prosperity over the next century. The phases of that growth, however, have to be deduced by the now wide-ly respected techniques of plan analysis. Research on Ludlow by W.H. St John Hope (1909) and E.G.R. Conzen (1968) played a significant part in the evolution of these techniques and the latter's postulation of Ludlow's 'plan units' as an index of urban development is a classic for the study of processes of urban growth. Conzen's work has been refined and amended by others, while the ways in which his phases of growth can be matched with documentary evidence has afforded scope for many interesting speculations.

Conzen postulated that the first phase of Ludlow's growth was the 'generously proportioned' High Street market place, running eastwards from the castle - which he termed 'the urban nucleus' - to meet the pre-existing north-south routeway at the Bull Ring. This plan unit consisted of the market place itself, which was seven perch-es wide, plus the burgages abutting on both sides. The town's first church and its churchyard were located at the north east end of this plan unit. This was already a hallowed site, being next to the ancient 'low'. The town thus had the castle at one end of the market place and the church at the other - a common kind of Norman plan, as at Pembroke, a roughly contemporary new town established after 1100 by Gilbert de Clare. It is reasonable to suppose that this linear town was the one known as Ludlow in 1138 - and that which may have been captured in 1139.

A later development, creating a 'T-shaped' plan with the earlier High Street as its stem, - like that still discernible at Farnham in Surrey - , was the burgaging of Old Street and Corve Street. The burgage pattern along Corve Street is still clearly visi-ble, but that in Old Street has been much distorted, partly by the super-imposition of the town wall in the later 13th century. It is known that burgages at the north end of Corve Street were there by 1186, and it is tempting to infer that the whole of this plan unit was in existence before that date, reflecting, perhaps, the expansion of the town in the stable conditions after 1154 provided by the firm rule of King Henry II.

Ludlow's most sophisticated planning occurs in what can be called 'the south-ern plan unit', a rectilinear system of streets and burgages on the sloping land between the High Street market place and the River Teme. As stressed by Conzen, the streets here are 'functionally differentiated'. The main residential streets are Broad Street and Mill Street, but these are linked by cross lanes, while narrow parallel streets give back access to properties. Some of these back lanes, such as Christ Croft in Dinham, became redundant at an early date, while others, such as that between Broad Street and Old Street, were truncated when the town walls were constructed. It is likely, too, that part of this complex was over-ridden when the wall of the outer bailey was built. The triangular shape of central Dinham, part of which was occupied by St Thomas's chapel, is probably a reflection of the curve of the river and of the town defences which followed it, later consolidated as the town wall. The date of this southern plan unit is uncertain, but it is tempting to see it as a late 12th century devel-opment, causing the rebuilding of the parish church in 1199.

The sequence of other planning phases is a matter for speculation. They include the burgaging of Upper and Lower Galdeford, and the laying out of a grid of four-perch burgages on the flood plains of Linney. Another development, probably under-way by 1200, is the infilling of parts of the High Street market place with rows of stalls which later became permanent buildings, and the narrowing of other parts by encroachment.

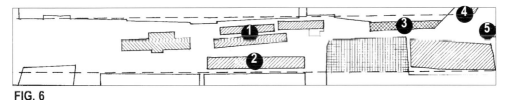

FIG. 6
The original High Street market place, as revealed on part of the 1885 1:500 O.S. map

— — — approximate lines of original street frontages.	**1** Shambles
wedge of southern plan unit into High Street, with later encroachment	**2** Barons's Row
	3 Taylors' Row
medieval infill	**4** The Shelde (from selda meaning stalls)
later infill	**5** The Tolsey (c15th)
infill against churchyard wall	

FIG. 7 Medieval Ludlow

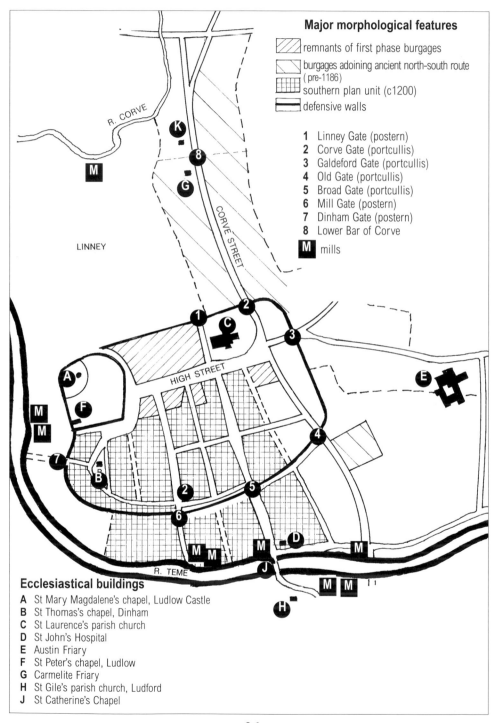

Major morphological features

- remnants of first phase burgages
- burgages adjoining ancient north-south route (pre-1186)
- southern plan unit (c1200)
- defensive walls

1 Linney Gate (postern)
2 Corve Gate (portcullis)
3 Galdeford Gate (portcullis)
4 Old Gate (portcullis)
5 Broad Gate (portcullis)
6 Mill Gate (postern)
7 Dinham Gate (postern)
8 Lower Bar of Corve

M mills

R. CORVE

CORVE STREET

LINNEY

HIGH STREET

R. TEME

Ecclesiastical buildings

A St Mary Magdalene's chapel, Ludlow Castle
B St Thomas's chapel, Dinham
C St Laurence's parish church
D St John's Hospital
E Austin Friary
F St Peter's chapel, Ludlow
G Carmelite Friary
H St Gile's parish church, Ludford
J St Catherine's Chapel

CHAPTER FOUR

1216-1461: A THRIVING MEDIEVAL TOWN

The people of Ludlow

In 1377 a surviving tax assessment record for English towns shows that Ludlow then had 1,172 adults and that it ranked 33rd among provincial towns. It was barely half the size of Shrewsbury, the county town, but was ahead of any other town in Shropshire and was larger than Southampton, Derby and Lichfield. The planning venture of the Lacys and their associates had clearly been successful and Ludlow's inclusion on the anonymous Gough map of 14th century Great Britain is an indication of its perceived status. In 1377 the town's total population of adults and children can be estimated at about 1,725, but in the late 13th century it had probably been more than 2,000, before the economic disasters of the mid-14th century. The Black Death of 1349 left many empty properties in Ludlow, perhaps as many as a third.

Detailed study of Ludlow in the reign of Richard II (1377-99) yields the remarkable total of 1,032 names. Many of these have only a single reference, such as Richard Heyton, leather-worker, but others occur frequently, for example Philip Lingen, merchant, who held important local offices, owned property in Old Street and traded as far afield as Coventry. Many people are known only through their crimes, for example John Rockhill, walker [fuller], charged with theft in 1375 and trespass in 1390. In some cases a surviving will gives glimpses of a person's life-style and character, as with Agnes de Hinswode whose will was made in 1379. She was an unmarried gentlewoman, with three servants and two houses, one of them in Mill Street. Her bequests include a best cloak, a robe with a red hood, a wine jar and silver spoons; and she made donations to 'the shrine of St Thomas in Hereford' and to 'poor husbandmen in the country', a reminder of the harsh economic conditions of the 1370s.

The lords of Ludlow and their castle

Many of the lords of Ludlow during these years were great men. They pursued their own interests ruthlessly, and were often involved in national politics. Ludlow was just part of the huge estates these lords accumulated - by inheritance, by conquest or by royal favour. Yet the well-defended castle at the heart of the Welsh Marches was a strategic asset while the need to maximise their incomes ensured that they and their agents promoted the town's economy when they were able to do so. At times, however, military reverses brought the town great hardship, as in 1459, when the Yorkists capitulated at the so-called battle of Ludford. The Lancastrians then sacked the town, so that 'men wente wetschode [wet-shod] in wynn [wine] ... and bare a-waye beddynge, clothe, and other stuffe, and defoulyd many wymmen'.

Walter, the last male Lacy, continued to spend much time in Ireland, one of his exploits being to invade Connaught in 1220. When he died, blind and infirm in 1241, his estates were divided between two young grand-daughters, Maud and Margery, who became wards of the king. The elder, Maud, became the wife first of Peter de Geneva and then of Geoffrey de Genevile, who came from Champagne. The younger, Margery, married John de Verdun of Alton, in Staffordshire. These were arranged marriages with persons whom the King, Henry III, wished to reward, for the estates involved were considerable. Both Peter de Geneva and Geoffrey de Genevile were courtiers attached to Elianor of Savoy, whom Henry had married in 1236, so that Ludlow played a part in cementing an important diplomatic marriage.

For many years after 1241 the manor of Ludlow was in two parts, held by the heirs of Maud and Margery. Some of the privileges of lordship were shared, such as the advowson, i.e. the presentation of a new Rector. The fact that these lords had interests far from Ludlow helped the town's burgesses to develop a large measure of

Fig. 8 shows the close links between the pedigree of the Mortimers and the Royal lineage of England. The recognition of the white Lion of March, an emblem of the Mortimers, as one of the six royal beasts acknowledges this relationship. Carvings of the royal beasts are at Kew Gardens and larger statues are erected at the entrance to Westminster Abbey for coronations.

Fig 8 Manorial Lords of Ludlow and their links with the Kings of England

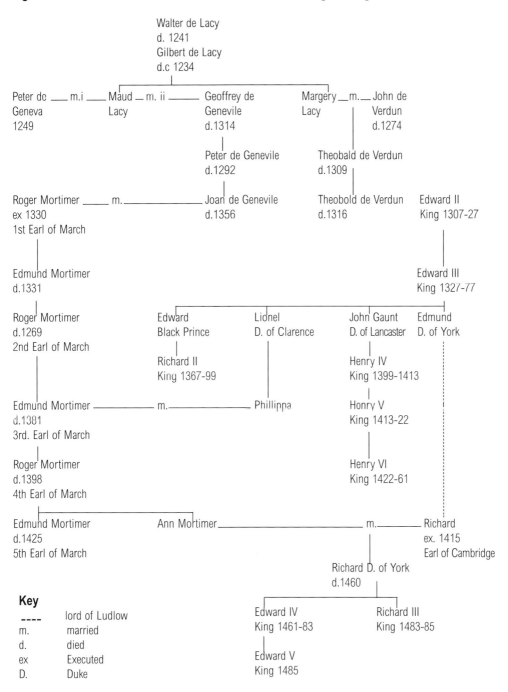

Key

----	lord of Ludlow
m.	married
d.	died
ex	Executed
D.	Duke

self-government, though an annual fee-farm rent had to be paid. Generally, the Verduns had little impact on the affairs of Ludlow, though the presence of their arms and those of related families in windows of the north aisle of St Laurence's suggest that they may have been benefactors when that part of the church was rebuilt. The Geneviles, however, were more closely involved, if only because their moiety included the castle.

Geoffrey de Genevile travelled extensively. He was with King Edward I on the third crusade and in Wales in 1282, when Edward started the campaign that led to the construction of Conway, Harlech and other castles around the Welsh heartland in Snowdonia. But like the Lacys, his major interest was in Ireland, where he became Justicar (Viceroy) in 1273. His base was at Trim, where he completed the keep and where he spent the last seven years of his life as a monk in a Dominican Friary – which he himself had endowed. Involvement abroad was the reason why in 1283 Geoffrey de Genevile gave Ludlow Castle and his moiety of the town to his son Peter. It was probably Peter who started to rebuild the domestic range along the north side of the inner bailey. The Welsh conquests of Edward I had brought more stable conditions to the Marches and these buildings helped to transform the castle from a military outpost into a fortified palace. The Geneviles stood high in royal favour and would have been eager to emulate the fashionable building styles of the day. It is likely that Peter commissioned the great first-floor hall – the venue for formal occasions and entertainments for the next three centuries – and the lower two storeys of the large solar or residential block to the west, together with the detached kitchen and other domestic buildings.

The keep of Trim Castle, started by the Lacys and finished by Geoffrey de Genevile

The domestic or north range of Ludlow Castle, photographed in 1976 during a Ludlow Festival performance of Hamlet. The buildings, erected by Peter Geneville and Roger Mortimer, provide a superb setting for historical drama. Lighting rigs are supported by the walls of the kitchen on the left and by the round nave of the Norman chapel of St Mary Magdalene on the right.

The most significant single event in the history of Ludlow castle is the marriage of Peter's daughter and heiress, Joan, to Roger Mortimer in 1307. The Mortimers, a Normandy family who had fought with William the Conqueror in 1066, had become lords of Wigmore, a few miles west of Ludlow, and this marriage was part of an upward spiral in their fortunes which eventually put the crown of England within their grasp. It was probably Roger who completed the western solar block and who then added the Great Chamber block to the east of the hall, with up-to-date ornamented fireplaces and other luxurious fittings.

The career of Roger Mortimer, related in Marlowe's Edward II, is the stuff that legends are made of. He and other barons opposed the weak rule of Edward II and his favourites. Captured in 1322 by Edward, who later occupied Ludlow Castle, Mortimer was imprisoned in the Tower of London, but escaped to France in 1324, reputedly drugging the guards. Here he became the ally and lover of Edward's estranged queen, Isabella, and together they led an army back to England which deposed the king, murdered him in Berkeley Castle, and installed the adolescent King Edward III on the throne but with Mortimer as chief adviser. This was the peak of his power. It was probably the time when he built the gardrobe (toilets) tower at Ludlow Castle, with its eight chambers with gardrobes - a remarkable en-suite facility for that period - and it is tempting to see him entertaining the court at Ludlow, perhaps in June 1328, when the King and his mother attended a great tournament at Hereford at the marriage of two of Mortimer's daughters. Later that year he was created Earl of March, by 'girding with the sword as the custom is'.

But 'proud Mortimer' quickly over-reached himself and antagonised powerful allies. Two years later he was seized at Nottingham and taken to an ignominious execution at Tyburn, where Marlowe has him proclaim:

And seeing there was no place to mount up higher,
Why should I greve at my declining fall?

The exterior of the Gardrobe Tower and adjoining buildings as portrayed on a 17th century picture of the castle. Each chamber had a window, as did four of the gardrobes. Beneath the windows can be seen the lavatorial shutes which emptied to the slopes below. To the left, the Tudor lodgings have a large oriel window, while one of the tall windows of the hall can be seen on the right.

For a generation the Mortimer ambition was spent, but the Earl's grandson, another Roger, gradually rebuilt the family fortunes, serving with distinction at Crecy in 1346, and winning back the Earldom of March in 1354. It was this Mortimer who completed a series of transactions begun by his grandfather to re-unite the manor of Ludlow, though some alienations to religious houses remained. It was the third Earl, Edmund, who revived the dynastic ambitions of the Mortimers by his marriage to Philippa, daughter of the King's eldest brother. In 1415, as Shakespeare reveals, this marriage was the justification of an unsuccessful bid for the throne on behalf of Edmund Mortimer, Philippa's grandson, on the grounds that Henry V, descended from a younger branch of the royal family, had an inferior claim. The plot was discovered and put down, but it was later taken up again by Richard Duke of York, who could claim descent from two royal lines, and whose mother, in the absence of a male heir, was the heiress of the Mortimers.

These dynastic wrangles were the excuse for the protracted struggles between rival groups of barons during the middle years of the 15th century, now remembered as the Wars of the Roses. Richard Duke of York, the leader of the Yorkists, had a high regard for Ludlow and in 1454 sent his sons, later Edward IV and Richard III, to be brought up at the castle, away from the intrigues of London. In October 1459, however, Ludlow itself was at the maelstrom of events, as the Lancastrians, led by the King, advanced from the south and camped at Ludford, with the Yorkist leaders and their armies assembled in the town. A great battle seemed imminent but during the night a large number of mercenaries deserted from the Yorkists to the Lancastrians. This created such disparity of numbers that Richard and Edward thought it wise to escape. Next day, 13 October, the Lancastrians had an easy victory at Ludford and went on to take the town. Seventeen months later, however, on 3 February, 1461, the Yorkists had their revenge at the battle of Mortimer's Cross ten miles south-west of Ludlow, one of a series of victories which led later that year to the crowning of Edward IV, great-nephew of the last male Mortimer, as King of England.

The government of Ludlow

Although no early charters survive, the town had powers of self-government by the mid-13th century or earlier. A body known as the Community of Burgesses was in existence by 1269 and accounts show that this body operated markets and fairs, and owned and repaired property. By 1308 'the Twelve', selected from the Community of Burgesses, were administering the town, while there are also references to a larger group called 'the Twenty Five'. In 1449, when the Duke of York confirmed the privileges of the borough, the 12 and 25 were described as having been chosen for 'good rule, consell and governance ... sythe the time that no mind is ...' Much of the work was undertaken by one or two bailiffs, but it is not known if they owed their first loyalties to the community or to the lords. Their surnames suggest that many of these bailiffs were local men, such as Hugh Cleyburi, bailiff in 1288, and a number of them were described as 'clerk', such as Richard Momele in 1271. By the later 14th century most of them were merchants, for example John Parys (d.1449), draper, owner of 'the house with the leaden porch' on the site of 18 Castle Street and donor of the 'Annunciation Window' in the parish church.

The early 15th century Tolsey or Toll-house in the Bull Ring, where the courts were held and the '12 and 25' had their meetings.

John Parys, draper, bailiff 1439-40 who would often have presided here. This stylised portrayal is from the Annunciation Window.

One major act of town government was the creation of the town walls. In 1233 it was recorded that 'the men of Ludlow have letters for the enclosure of their town', but there is no evidence of work on the walls until 1260, when Geoffrey de Genevile was granted a murage. i.e. the right to levy taxes, 'to repair the walls of Ludlow'. The wording suggests that parts of the wall, at least, were already in place, perhaps as earth ramparts, though their relationship to the town plan has yet to be established. The 1260 grant came at a time of danger on the Welsh border, following seizure of power in south Wales in 1255 by Llewelyn ap Gruffudd.

A series of further murages show that the construction and repair of the walls continued for many years, but title deeds and other evidence suggest that most parts of the system were in place by 1270 or a little earlier. The walls, of stone, are about a mile in circumference, and were crenellated in at least some places. They still survive for about two-thirds of their length, though often mutilated and restored. In height and thickness, however, they did not compare with the walls surrounding larger places such as Canterbury or York. There were seven gates, four of which - Broad Gate, Corve Gate, Galdeford Gate and Old Gate - had twin drum towers in the style of the castle towers built in North Wales in the years after 1270. The walls and gates clearly had a defensive function but they also ensured that people entering the town used the gates where tolls could be collected. Parts of the town were outside the walls but 'the lower bar of Corve' gave some protection to Corve Street and its burgages.

This 1719 view of Galdford Tower suggests it may have incorporated Galdeford Gate, though documents indicate that they were adjacent.

The Broad Gate in 1824, showing a large 18th century house above a medieval gateway. The smaller houses are in the town ditch.

A frontal view in 1721 of Dinham Gate, one of the small postern gates. Drawn by antiquarian William Stukeley.

The construction and maintenance of the mills was another important function of town government, for only the lord or a body such as the community of burgesses had the capital to finance such enterprises. The number of mills at Ludlow - some used for corn, others for fulling - grew rapidly in the early 13th century. The most ambitious scheme was the construction of what is now called 'the horseshoe weir' downstream from Ludford bridge. This powered the mill at the bottom of Old Street, known for many years as 'the New Mill', and the mills at Ludford. In 1241 the ownership of four mills - two at Mill Street, two at Old Street - was divided between the daughters of Walter Lacy, one of these moieties later passing to the Convent of Aconbury, near Hereford. A mill at Steventon, called the Sheet Mill, was also in existence during the reign of Henry III (1216-1272), while there were smaller mills on the River Corve and on a outlet from the Corve in Linney. The last two mills to be developed were probably in Dinham below the castle, but by 1368 these were the most important corn mills in Ludlow.

The construction of 'the Horseshoe Weir', photographed by Francis Bedford in the 1870s, was an impressive feat of hydraulic engineering. The stone and timber-framed building on the right marks the site of two medieval fulling mills, were the cloth was cleansed and beaten. These mills were given to the Palmers' Guild in 1349 and 1350 after the Black Death. The buildings of the Old Street mills, rebuilt to a plan of Thomas Telford in 1810, can be seen on the left.

Markets and Fairs

The weekly market, held on Thursdays, was central to Ludlow's economy, as perceived by Margery de Stretford, who stated at the Assizes in 1368 that: 'Ludlow is a market town ... since time out of mind ...' People poured in from the countryside to trade, to socialise and sometimes to fight, as in 1255 when 'Philip le Lou of Stokesay and Walter Scyre of Clunton came from the market place of Ludlow and Philip struck Walter on the head from which he died.' Court records also give information about produce, as in 1372, when wine, fish, salt and herrings were taken from the cart of 'the Abbot of Redynge', probably destined for Leominster Priory, a daughter house of Reading Abbey.

The annual fairs drew people from much further afield. Because each moiety of the manor had its own fair or fairs, it is uncertain which fair is the oldest, but this is likely to be that of May 1st, held on the feast of St Philip and St James, to whom the parish church was originally dedicated. St Laurence's Fair, on 9,10 and 11 August, probably goes back to the time when the dedication changed to St Laurence, perhaps after the rebuilding of 1199. It was certainly in existence in 1274, when a gatekeeper detained two men of Cleobury who refused to pay toll on oxen bought at the fair. A third fair, that of St Catherine on 24, 25 and 26 November, was added by charter in 1328.

This view of a French bishop blessing a local fair shows many features which would have been familiar at Ludlow: the flock of sheep, the bales of wool and the small shops and taverns, in some of which business is being transacted.

Farming and food supply

Medieval people lived closer to nature than we do and the weather and the yield of the harvest were reflected in prices. A local chronicler recorded that there were 'vast amounts' of wheat in 1288, when a bushel sold for 2d., in contrast to the high costs of the early 14th century, when corn was 20d a bushel in 1315, 30d in 1316 and 40d in 1322. These higher costs reflected growing demand due to increasing population, as well as harvest failure and animal diseases. Crops grown locally included wheat, oats and peas, all listed in 1331 among the goods of the late Earl of March and of his widow. Cultivation took place on 'the open fields of Ludlow', which stretched as far as Prior's Halton in the west, Stanton Lacy in the north, Rock in the east and Overton in the south.

Many Ludlow burgesses owned animals, such as Philip de Cheyne, merchant,

from whom 'two horses, two mares, eight cows and three bullocks worth £20' were stolen in 1327. Animals were grazed on Whitcliffe, the closes in Linney and along what is now Fishmore - then Fishpool Lane. The steep slopes below the castle were also used, the bailiffs' accounts of 1368 recording '3s. from the pastures of the castle motte'. The importance of finding pasture caused many disputes, as in 1221 when the Abbot of Gloucester, who owned much of Whitcliffe, was at variance with the burgesses of Ludlow. This led to the purchase of grazing rights on Whitcliffe from the manors of Bromfield and Ludford. Both the Abbot and Jordan of Ludford were given the right to trade at Ludlow market free of toll, but the Abbot had the right to use the stone quarries and to receive four pence of wax yearly, as against a cash payment to Jordan of 100s.

The cow in this 15th century picture from a chancel window in the parish church is reputed to be the earliest known portrayal of the Hereford breed.

The tradesmen and their guilds

An indication of the many trades practised in medieval Ludlow is given by 'trade' surnames, which account for about a third of all known names. The earliest rental of the Palmers Guild, for example, compiled in the mid-13th century, has more than 80 such names. Not all those who bore such names were still practising the trade, but their forbears had probably done so, two or three generations back. Names such as

Reginald Fuller, John Scherman [Shearman] and William Scissor testify to the early importance of cloth manufacture, but the overall impression is one of a great range of trades. Names like 'Grinder', 'Loker' (locksmith), 'Typper' (arrowhead maker) and 'Furbiser' (armourer) show that there were many metal trades on the still-troubled Welsh border, while names such as 'Furminager' (cheesemonger), 'Haranc' (fishdealer) and 'Huny' (honey) indicate some of the products which could be purchased. The name 'Moneter' (money-dealer) occurs five times, suggesting commercial transactions, while names like 'Hugh the Mason' show that building was an important activity. Some tradesmen no doubt still practised the trades from which they took their names, for example 'Symon the Mercer', who had a shop in Drapers or Mercers Row (now King Street).

Simon the Apostle in a window in St John's Chapel, shown as a carpenter with a saw.

The tradesmen organised themselves into craft guilds, otherwise known as Companies or Fellowships. In 1368, 14 guilds disputed the order of precedence in a Corpus Christi day procession, an occasion of public ritual and celebration. It was agreed that the shoemakers, who seem to have been the agitators, should come 10th of the 13 crafts which preceded the shrine, the merchants occupying the prestigious position behind the shrine. Generally, the food trades were at the front and the cloth and leather-making trades in the middle, while the tailors, skinners and drapers, who later amalgamated to form the powerful Guild of Stitchmen, were all towards the rear. A notable omission is the group of metal, wood and building trades later known as 'the Companie of Smiths or Hammermen'.

Wool collection and marketing

Much of Ludlow's medieval wealth came from the collection and marketing of wool. Britain produced the world's finest wool and the most highly priced came from the Welsh border. Sheep thrived in the hill country around Ludlow, such as the nine flocks, each of about 240 animals, managed for the Earl of Arundel in the lordship of Clun.

Merchants based at Ludlow were in a prime position to collect wool and market it, elsewhere in England and abroad. Those licensed to export wool during the reign of Edward I included Nicholas Gow, Thomas Erlich, Thomas de Langeford, William de Orleton and Philip de Wigmore, all 'merchants of Ludlow'. There were also grants to Nicholas de Ludlow, described as 'the King's Merchant', and his son Laurence de Ludlow. Both are described as 'of Shrewsbury', but the family owned property in Ludlow. When Laurence was drowned at sea in 1294, whilst exporting wool, a chronicler described him as 'the most renowned of merchants', and added that his body 'was carried to Ludlow and there taken to burial', a strong indication of his birth in the town. The manor house at Stokesay, which he rebuilt and which he had permission to crenellate in 1291, is a standing memorial to the wealth of Ludlow's 13th century wool trade.

This prosperity continued into the 14th century. Some Ludlow merchants spent time abroad, as in 1332, when Nicholas Erlich and others, accused of taking wool from a Bridgnorth merchant, were described as 'English merchants dwelling in Brugges'. Wool from Ludlow went as far afield as Florence, for in 1345 Roger, son of Walter de Deghere of Ludlow, was in dispute with the powerful Pucci family of that city.

Cloth manufacture

As in many towns, cloth manufacture became of increasing importance in the 14th century and after 1400 it became Ludlow's leading industry. Of 221 persons with known occupations engaged in litigation between 1400 and 1449, 69, i.e. 31%, were engaged in cloth making and another 12 (6%) in trades which used cloth. The beginnings of the industry, however, go back to at least the 1220's, when there was a fulling mill at the bottom of Broad Street, adjoining Ludford Bridge. This fulling mill, the earliest recorded in Shropshire, was a product of what has been called 'the first technological revolution', which from about 1180 caused the later processes of cloth manufacture to be located where water power was available. Ludlow, with its fast flowing rapids, was well able to benefit from this development.

Cloth manufacture was a vertically integrated industry, with a range of specialist craftsmen. For Ludlow, least is known about the preliminary processes of carding – disentangling the fibres – and spinning, much of which probably took place in the surrounding countryside. But the town did have some cardmakers, such as Thomas

This view to the north east from the tower of the parish church clearly shows the burgages on the east side of Corve Street, beyond which were 'the yards' where cloth was dried and stretched on tenterers' racks. The racks extended up the slope of what is now called Gravel Hill, creating a billowing mass of white and coloured cloth – one of the distinctive sights of Ludlow and other cloth-producing towns.

Bridewoode in 1413. The weavers, however, were a prominent local group, including men like Walter Codur, who died in 1449, who had been Bailiff 1437–39, and again in 1440. Men of his standing probably employed others to weave cloth and used their own energies for marketing. His son, William Codur, was a merchant at Bristol, an important trading outlet for the valleys of the Severn and its tributaries. Walter Codur was one of the successful Ludlovians of his day, and a road on Ludlow's new business park was recently named after him.

The woven cloth was subjected to various finishing processes, beginning with fulling, by which it was thickened, felted, and de-greased, using fuller's earth. Originally this was done by trampling the sodden cloth in tubs, so that 'walker'became a synonym for 'fuller', but later the larger operators used water power to drive hammers which pounded the cloth. Several mills along the Teme were adapted for this process, including those at Ludford and Steventon.

The cloth was dried and teased to raise a nap, and large shears were used to give a smooth finish. These stages were carried out by the shearmen, a trade that gave its name to one of Ludlow's most influential families, the Shermans, who owned land in Dinham and elsewhere. The cloth was then stretched and shaped on great racks by the process known as 'teyntering'. Lines of racks, with hanging cloths, were a familiar sight in late medieval Ludlow, especially on the south side of the town outside the Town Walls, and in 'the yards' which were east of what is now Portcullis Lane. A final stage was dyeing, using imported substances, such as the madder and alum brought for 87s by Walter Codur from a London supplier in 1443.

A fuller's club, shown in one of the windows of the parish church. It was used to pound cloth.

Especially after 1400, Ludlow cloth was widely marketed by the cloth merchants or clothiers who by then dominated the industry. The extent of the trading network is shown by court records, most of them concerning debts. By the late 14th century Ludlow drapers were being owed money from towns in adjoining counties, as in 1393, when Henry Kyngstone of Ludlow, draper, was owed £40 by William Stretton of Bridgnorth. By the 1420s a range of Ludlow cloths was on sale in London, as in 1421, when 16 wide cloths of 'blewmedlie' were valued at £37 6s 8d, and 15 whole cloths of 'a derkgrenemedle' at £37 10s. Trading links with London were strong. One merchant with whom Ludlow burgesses did business was Richard Whittington, mercer - better known as Dick Whittington. Quantities of Ludlow cloths were also sold to overseas merchants, as in 1422, when 'ten woollen cloths of Ludlow of diverse colours' were sold to a Genoese merchant for £40.

There is no doubt that the cloth industry thrived during these years, and that much of the profit came back to the town and its public institutions. The most obvious instance is the parish church, largely rebuilt after 1433 in the Perpendicular style of the day. The soaring tower of St Laurence's is still the town's best known landmark - the fifteenth century clothiers could have no finer memorial.

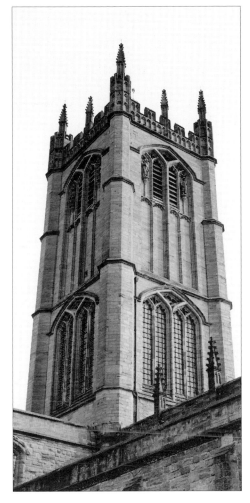

The tower of St Laurence's, built between c.1450 and 1471. Those who contributed included Richard Knyghtone (d.1466), who left 20 shillings:

For the meritorious work of the new building of the bell tower of the said church for the health of my soul and that of Margery my late wife, my parents, my children and my benefactors.

An age of faith

This was a time when Christian belief was central to people's outlook about this world and the hereafter. Almost all Ludlovians went to church on Sundays and holy days. Those who could afford to do so made generous bequests to church buildings and to spiritual causes. In 1321, John Ace left 10s. to the high altar of St Laurence's for his tithes, 2s. for 'adorning the rest of the altars', and 6s 8d 'for the subsidy to the Holy Land'. All believed in the power of prayer, as seen in the will of William de Pyrefield, made in 1348, on the eve of the Black Death. He left £40 of silver to 16 chaplains 'to celebrate masses for my soul and the souls of my parents and of Julian my wife, of John my son ... and of all the departed faithfull'. Many Ludlovians made elaborate provision for their funerals, seen as their entry into the next world. In 1304, Agnes Orm provided for 24 lbs of wax candles to be burnt around her body, left fees for the chaplains who attended, and gave ld. to each of the 60 clerks singing psalms for her soul. In the fifteenth century Ludlovians such as John Hereford in 1439 left their souls 'to Almighty God, the Blessed Virgin Mary and all the saints'. Saints were seen as those who had overcome human frailties and were now in the heavenly court, able to intercede for those still on earth. In the chancel of St Laurence's, alone, 34 saints are represented, including ten from the Roman Empire and two others from Europe, the medieval church transcending national boundaries. Pilgrimages to the shrines of saints were commonplace, such as that of Henry Herdeley in 1358 to the relics of St James at Santiago de Compostela in Spain.

St Catherine of Alexandria, who was martryed in the early fourth century, was a popular saint in Ludlow.

The institution which provided these services was the church. Its power was considerable and those who flouted its authority faced excommunication and often secular penalties as well. In 1347, for example, John Keek, Margery Neal and six other Ludlow persons had persisted in excommunication for forty days and more 'in contempt of the church', causing the Bishop of Hereford, having 'no further weapons', to apply to the King to have them 'whipped in chains and fetters until the injuries of the church are settled'.

The parish church

The church rebuilt in 1199 served the needs of Ludlow for over two hundred years, though a number of changes were made, using contemporary architectural styles, and reflecting the aspirations of the day.

In the 13th century, when members of the Ludlow family and other merchants were accumulating their wealth, a chancel was added to accommodate the High Altar, and a new south doorway was inserted. It is not known what the chancel looked like, but the south doorway is one of the gems of the present building. This beautifully moulded feature, in a pure Early English style, was rated as 'one of the most charming features of the church' by the late Dr Cranage.

The early fourteenth century brought continuing prosperity to Ludlow and with it the rebuilding of the north aisle. The Llandaff Chronicle, compiled about 1338, probably at Wigmore Abbey, records that in 1305 'the north aisle of the church of Ludelowe was made, which was finished in the third year following'. The window tracery and the ball flower ornamentation are characteristic of the more exuberant Decorated style which was then fashionable.

At about the same time, the hexagonal south porch was built. Its bold use of space catches the spirit of the Decorated style. The only other such porches in England are at Chipping Norton, another cloth town, and at St Mary Redcliffe, Bristol, a port with close trade links with Ludlow. The south transept was added about 1340, but the north transept is later, a monument to Ludlow's recovery from the Black Death of 1349.

The church as it stands today is largely the creation of the mid-fif-

The south porch, drawn by Buckler in 1822. The upper storey was called 'the parvis room', parvis coming form an old French word meaning paradise. Its purpose in the Middle Ages is not certain, but after the reformation it was occupied by a deacon, Thomas Higgs, who was 100 when he died in 1606. Buckler's drawing shows an outside entrance, now removed, to the access staircase.

teenth century, a time when the town enjoyed another bout of prosperity, and benefited from the patronage of Richard Duke of York and his allies. Between 1433 and 1471 the entire central part of the church was completely rebuilt. This only came about, however, after a bitter dispute between John Donwode, Rector from 1420, and his parishioners. The parishioners complained that the Rector was refusing to discharge his responsibility 'to repair the chancel of the church'. There must have been months of acrimony and frustration before they took the ultimate step open to them, an appeal to the Pope in Rome, a measure which led to the removal of Donwode by the gift of an enhanced pension, and a faculty for rebuilding in 1433.

The rebuilding was done in the soaring Perpendicular style of the day, a style which relied heavily on vertical emphasis. The late Alec Clifton Taylor wrote of the 'magnificence, stateliness, even a nobility' of great Perpendicular churches, and St Laurence's has been much admired for these qualities. John Leland recorded in 1539 that: 'There is but one church in the town but that is very fayr and large and richly adorned and taken for the fayrest in all these quarters'.

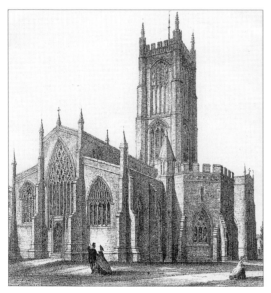

These lithographs drawn by E.H.Buckler soon after the 1859-60 restoration show the massive scale and fine proportions of St Laurence's. In the fifteenth century, the nave and aisles were cluttered with chantry chapels and dominated by a huge crucifix above the rood screen.

A panel from a window in St John's chapel, showing a procession led by a crucifer, followed by acolytes, the holy water sprinkler, chanters with their books, choristers and two pilgrims.

The pieta on one of the bench ends, showing a sorrowful Mary holding the broken body of Christ the redeemer. Christ's passion and death were central to medieval devotion.

Another bench end, showing the Lord of Misrule, appointed to preside over celebrations and festivities, especially at Christmas. This was one of many pagan rituals condoned by the church.

St Laurence's is a treasure house of artistic achievement over several centuries, but many of the finest creations date from the mid-fifteenth century. A number of these give us glimpses of the faith and customs of that time.

The names of eighteen Rectors have been traced for this period, beginning with William de Rumily, who was inducted in 1224. Some of these, like Robert Faryngton in 1371, held the benefice for short periods only as incidents in careers elsewhere, but others were based at Ludlow, including John de Vaucoulers, who was commended by the King in 1295 for residing in his church for seven years. However, much of the work of the parish was undertaken by other priests such as John Heyer, described as 'parish chaplain of Lodelowe' in 1427.

Small chapels and holy crosses

The presence of a number of small chapels and wayside crosses in and around Ludlow confirms the importance of religion in the medieval town. The three chapels founded in the twelfth century - St Mary Magdalene in the castle, St Thomas in Dinham and St Leonard in Corve Street - were augmented by two others later in the Middle Ages: that of St Peter in the outer bailey of the castle in 1328 and that of St Catherine on Ludford Bridge before 1406. St Peter's Chapel, the ruins of which now adjoin part of the public walk around the castle, is a link with the castle's heyday, for it was founded by Roger Mortimer to commemorate his escape from the Tower of London on St Peter's day, 1323. Two crosses, that of St Kellem and the Weeping Cross, were on the south-east boundary of Ludlow, the former where the parishes of Ludlow, Stanton Lacy and Ludford met at the north end of Weeping Cross Lane; and the latter where that lane met the River Teme. The chapels on the edge of the town - St Leonard in the north, Dinham in the west and St Catherine in the south - were no doubt used by travellers leaving or entering Ludlow, as well as by local residents. The crosses were also used by travellers and for meetings, while the Weeping Cross had its own penetential purposes.

What the Weeping Cross may have looked like, as in papers left by a 19th century antiquarian.

St Catherine's chapel was occupied in 1406 by Thomas Shelve of Leintwardine, a resident hermit. There are occasional hints at the arrangements for providing chaplains, as in 1404, when the Rector, John Piers, held the chaplaincy of St Mary Magdalene in the castle. Several early wills leave bequests for the fabric of one of the chapels. In 1381 William Pope, who owned property 'outside the bar of Corve', left 10s. 'to the chapel of St Leonard ... to repair it', while in 1410 John Marshetone, chaplain, who probably lived in Dinham, left 40d. 'to the fabric of the church of St Thomas the Martyr'. A different kind of gift was that of a 30 gallon lead vessel, made in 1349 to St Thomas's by Henry Weolere.

Hospitals and friaries

Under the umbrella of the church, hospitals were founded in many towns to give succour to the sick and the poor and also, in some cases, hospitality to travellers. Of eight known hospitals in Shropshire, two faced each other across Ludford Bridge: the leper hospital of St Giles of Ludford to the south and the Hospital of St John the Baptist to the north. Little is known about St Giles, but the four large chimneys of its successor, Ludford House, may be the legacy of a large residential institution. Leprosy was certainly a problem locally in 1309, when Ludlow burgesses arranged a collection for those afflicted; while in 1330 Henry Burway of Ludlow left 4d. 'to the Brethren of the lepers of Lodeford'. Another hostel, traditionally for pilgrims to St Winifred's well in north Wales, may have been Barnaby House, a large stone building which was later a town house for the Barnaby family of Lower Brockhampton.

More is known about the endowment of St John's, though rather less about its early work. It was founded early in the 13th century by Peter Undergood, a Ludlow burgess, who endowed it with local estates, including the early fulling mill in Lower Broad Street, acquired from the Lacys. Many other properties were granted later, including Ludford manor and two more mills, and over 40 burgages in Ludlow. Some of these were between Lower Broad Street and Frog Lane, from which the Hospital developed a precinct, including its own cemetery. In the 15th century, however, the Hospital seems to have been principally a small college of priests, which enjoyed the patronage of the Mortimers. In 1458 'the free chapel in Ludlow castle' was united to it 'on condition that intercession for the souls of the Duke of York and his kindred are incessantly offered'.

Some of the early functions of the hospitals were probably taken over by friars, who swept across England from 1221, committed to preaching, poverty and scholarship. The Dominicans were at Shrewsbury by 1232 and the Franciscans there and at Bridgnorth in the 1240s; but it was a community of Austin friars - locally called 'the black friars' - who came first to Ludlow in 1254, moving from an earlier rural location near Cleobury Mortimer. The last friary to be set up in Shropshire was also at Ludlow, in 1350, in the grim months after the Black Death, one of the last foundations by the Carmelites or white friars, who already had 35 English houses.

The Austin friars' first house was probably on the redundant street in Dinham which perhaps acquired its name, Christ Croft, because of this association. This was demesne land, held directly under one of the manorial lords, probably a sponsor of their coming to Ludlow. In 1256 they moved to nine burgages in Lower Galdeford, and in 1284 the ancient route along what is still called Friars' Walk was diverted to enlarge this site. Early benefactors included Brian de Brampton, lord of Kinlet. Another landowner, Laurence de Ludlow of Stokesay,

A tentative reconstruction of the Austin Friary by the Ludlow architect Herbert Evans, based on excavations in 1861. The long church is across the top of the picture, with the bell tower at the corner of the chancel. The conventual buildings are to the south, with the refectory facing the church.

grandson of the rich wool merchant, was the principal benefactor of the Carmelites in 1350. Perhaps seeking atonement for earlier crimes - he had been outlawed for assault in 1346 - he granted eight properties in Corve Street 'for a ... habitation ... of new building'.

It can be assumed that the friars brought new fervour to the religious life of Ludlow. Six of ten Ludlow wills proved between 1300 and 1350 had money bequests to the Austin Friars while in the 1380s three benefactors left substantial sums to both houses. After 1400, however, gifts are very rare, reflecting the completion of building but also, to a degree, a decline in popularity, as the friars' standards became less stringent. Both friaries eventually had huge churches, the size of the naves suggesting that large congregations came to hear the preaching for which the friars were famous. Some friars achieved distinction, among them Robert Mascall, a Carmelite Prior who became Bishop of Hereford in 1406. Scandals were not unknown, as in 1445, when Thomas Eaton, a Carmelite, was charged with fornication. Generally, however, the reputations of both houses were good. The Austin Friary was one of the order's leading houses in England and a provincial chapter was held there in 1426. The Carmelites' great moment came in 1452, when King Henry VI and his queen spent the night there, spurning his rival at the castle, Richard Duke of York.

Palmers' Guild

The earliest references to the Palmers Guild are title deeds of the mid–13th century, which bequeath rent charges on Ludlow properties to 'the Blessed Mary and the Brotherhood of the Palmers' Guild'. The instigator was probably Geoffrey Andrew, a member of a wealthy, property-owning Ludlow family, who was the first known Warden, from the late 1250s to his death before 1284. Though sometimes used as a general term for pilgrim, a 'palmer' meant specifically a pilgrim to the Holy Land, who had returned with a palm-branch or palm-leaf as evidence of his journey. It is possible that Geoffrey Andrew himself had been to the Holy Land before Jerusalem had fallen to the Muslims in 1244. An alternative view is that he was influenced by the growing cult of Edward the Confessor, who was linked to palmers in a legend then gaining widespread currency - and which the Guild was later to adopt and display in a 15th century window in the parish church. The main purpose of the Guild was to support priests to intercede for the souls of living and dead members. A gift to the Guild by Geoffrey Andrew of an annual rent charge of 12d., payable for ever from one of his Ludlow properties, has the preamble: I, with charitable intent have given and granted ... for the good of my soul and of the soul of all my predecessors and successors, in pure, free and perpetual alms, for the perpetual maintenance of a chaplain for God and the blessed Mary, serving in the church of Lodelowe. The Guild also provided fellowship for its members, and served, in a pre-Welfare State age, as a mutual benefit society, with relief for those who had suffered from poverty, fire, shipwreck and other misfortunes.

This panel from the Palmers' window in St Laurence's parish church shows two Ludlow pilgrims, hands raised in prayer, embarking on a pilgrimage in a 15th century vessel.

The names of many early members are included in a list of 113 rent charges donated to the Guild in mid-13th century, all of them Ludlow residents. The Guild was controlled by an elected Council, which eventually had twelve members, many of whom also held positions of secular authority in the town. The head of the Guild was a Warden, who usually held office for life, assisted by one or two stewards, and by a clerk, the first known being Walter of Hopton, 1293-1308. The Guild was financed by subscriptions and by receipts from properties, most of these being rent charges in the early days. The Guild employed two chaplains in 1270 but the number had risen by 1349 when Henry le Weolers, making his will when the Black Death was at its peak, left 2d. each to 'seven priests of the Palmers' Guild'. All or nearly all Guild members during its first century were local residents; by the later 14th century some came from further afield, including Bristol and Chester, though these may have been relatives of Ludlow families or emigrants from the town.

Religious guilds such as the Palmers occurred in most English towns, meeting a largely local need. In the 1390s, however, the Palmers assumed a regional, almost a national function, rather as nineteenth century building societies, like the Halifax, later became much more than local institutions. A number of prominent land-owners around the town, such as Sir Hugh Cheney of Cheney Longville and John Burley of Broncroft, became members while 15th century enrolments included Richard Duke of York. By the 1430s members came from all over Shropshire and adjoining countries, as well as from Bristol and London, with the Guild stewards undertaking journeys each year through southern England and Wales to recruit and collect subscriptions. The Guild derived enhanced prosperity from this increased membership and also from the practice of individuals endowing daily masses or annual obits for the benefit of themselves and their families. The first of these was in 1393, when Hugh Ace, Vicar of St Katherine's, Hereford, a member of a long established family of Ludlow merchants, left properties in Ludlow to Guild trustees so that they may:

> ... solemnly make and arrange ... the annual anniversary for the souls of William my father, Isabell my mother, Philip my brother and of me the said Sir Hugh Ace on the Feast of the Assumption of the Blessed Virgin Mary ...

The expansion of the Guild resulted in an impressive building programme, beginning in 1393-94 with the erection of a College, where the priests of the Guild, previously in lodgings, could live. The College resembled an Oxbridge quadrangle, with buildings around the courtyard. An eastern range fronting College Street had a hall to the north and a kitchen to the south, where a huge chimney can still be detected. The Guild's social and administrative centre was in Mill Street, where an earlier

Guildhall was rebuilt in 1411, part of a courtyard complex with a barn and gatehouse. Much of the Guildhall is still standing, though masked by its brick casing of 1768. It takes the form of a massive aisled hall, a prestigious style of building matched in the central Marches only by the Bishop's Palace at Hereford. Here a grand Pentecostal Feast was held, with wine imported from Bordeaux. The arcades on each side of the central nave supported an ornate and richly timbered roof, part of which is now hidden above the inserted eighteenth century ceiling.

The Mill Street elevation of the Guildhall, with the asymmetrical position of the doorway giving a clue that the Georgian facade masks an earlier building.

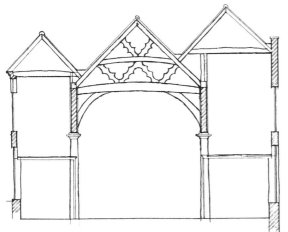

This section of the Guildhall shows the central nave. A curved suspended ceiling now obscures the upper part of the roof from public view.

The Guild continued to accumulate properties, some of them by purchase, and there was a sustained programme of building and repair. By 1439 annual income exceeded £85, coming from 167 rent charges, 96 tenements, 30 shops and 18 other properties, including one fulling mill. One Guild property was 'the corner shop' (now Bodenham's) at the top of Broad Street, where four small shops, acquired before 1392, were absorbed into a three storey jettied building erected by the Guild in 1403-04. By the 1440s the fortunes of the Guild were riding high. Their activities were a social focus for the better-off citizens of Ludlow. Their Wardens were among the richest and most influential local men of their time, e.g. William Paris, Warden c.1422 to 1440, a rich draper and cloth merchant, who had been Bailiff 1416-19.

A reconstruction of the 15th century 'corner shop'.

By the 1430s the Guild had taken responsibility for the teaching of grammar in Ludlow and in the 1440s they contributed generously to the rebuilding of the parish church. In the church they now had special use of the chapel of St John the Evangelist, a saint often included in the dedications of the Guild and who played a central role in the legend of the Palmers and Edward the Confessor. The mid-fifteenth century window in the chapel which relates that legend and uses it to attribute the charter of the Guild to Edward Confessor – two centuries before its foundation and nearly three centuries before the actual incorporation in 1329 – is an imaginative device to enhance the authority and credibility of the Guild. The report of John Leland in 1540 suggests this had been to a large degree successful, though the astute chronicler himself clearly had some reservations:

> Thise churche hathe bene much avauncyd by a brothar-hode therein foundyd in the name of St John the Evangeliste.
> The originall thereof was (as the people say there) in the tyme of K.Edward the Confessor and it is constantly affirmyd there that the pilgrimes, that browght the ringe from beyond the se as a token from St John thevangelist to Kyne Edward, were inhabituants of Ludlow.

The Palmers Window

This has eight panels, the last two of which are reproduced here.
The missing panels show:

1 Palmers embarking on a pilgrimage (see p.51).
2 King Edward the Confessor giving a ring to St John, disguised as a beggar.
3 St John, no longer disguised, asking the Palmers to return the ring to King Edward, saying he will be in paradise in six months.
4 The Palmers give the ring to the King.
5 A procession of celebration (see p. 47).
6 The King gives the Palmers their Guild charter.

The panels here show:

7 (left): The Palmers are welcomed at one of the Ludlow gates by a Bailiff. The gate and people are stylised but there would have been watchers, as in the tower above the gate.
8 (right): A celebration in the Guildhall. A harpist entertains while the greyhound is the badge of the Earl of Warwick, an ally of Richard Duke of York, a Guild member and patron.

55

Buildings

Medieval Ludlow had more than 500 burgage plots, as well as the large spaces occupied by the castle and the parish church. It is likely that some plots, especially those in Linney, never had buildings on them, while by the mid-15th century or earlier others, such as those on the south side of what is now Camp Lane, had been merged into small enclosed fields. On the other hand, a number of burgages contained more than one building, as on the south side side of Lower Galdeford, where three adjoining plots had 16 cottages and a dovecote, as well as an orchard.

Some of the earliest buildings were of stone and timber. There is twelfth century or earlier stonework at the castle, St Thomas's chapel and the parish church. The most common Ludlow stone is a rough, chunky, calcareous siltstone, from the quarries on Whitcliffe and elsewhere. This material does not weather well, however, so pink sandstone from Old Red Sandstone quarries east of the town was used when stronger masonry was needed. Though indifferently served by stone, Ludlow had easy access to supplies of timber, as in 1418, when four large oaks for beams and wallplates were brought to the castle 'from Madiknell Wood', probably the area now called Mary Knoll, about two miles west of the town. Standing buildings show that box frame construction was commonly used, though there are documentary references to crucks, i.e. pairs of curved timbers taken from the same tree. These were sometimes called 'forks', as in 1271, when Peter Gelemin was crushed by a 'fork', the value of which was 6d. Some items had to be imported, as shown by Palmers' Guild accounts of the 1420s, when 9s. was paid 'to John Gregory of Sturbridge for 3,000 boardnails'. These accounts, which cover the building of five houses, show the relative importance of different kinds of craftsmen.

Of some 1,500 days worked, more than a third were by carpenters and sawyers, compared with five percent by masons and stone cutters, supporting other indications that most houses at this time were timber framed. The fact that tilers worked 393 days, compared with only 43 by thatchers, suggests that roofs were more often tiled than thatched. Of 24 craftsmen named, the most important was John Baldesley, probably the leading carpenter in Ludlow at this time. On a house next to Galdeford Gate, Baldesley worked 63 days, but at various times no less than 17 other men also worked there, including tilers for 16 days, perhaps on the main roof, and thatchers for five days, perhaps on an out-house roof.

Especially near the town centre, and along Corve Street and Broad Street, many of the land-holdings or tenements consisted of groups of buildings, some of which were domestic, others agricultural or commercial. In 1325 a legal dispute involved a tenement with a room, a kitchen, a malt kiln and a barn. In 1349 Simon Plotemon left 'my hall kitchen and grange' to his wife, then to his son. In 1392 Thomas de Pauntley was accused of wasting a property let to him by St John's Hospital which contained a hall, a kitchen, two stables and a bakehouse. Other holdings were smaller, such as the 38 'cottages' listed in a Palmers' Guild rental of 1439, most of these being in Mill Street, Old Street, Frog Lane (now St John's Lane) and 'Narrowlane' (now Raven Lane). A Guild rental of c.1290 lists twenty 'selda' or single storey shops, but by 1439 18 of the 34 'selda' owned by the Guild had 'solars above', i.e. private living rooms where the family could be 'alone'. This suggests that many traders and their families were now living 'over the shop'.

The hall and other rooms

The most important room in a medieval house was the hall, originally synonymous with 'house' or 'living space'. In larger houses, with no site restrictions, there were normally more private rooms at the 'upper end', often a parlour below and a solar or chamber above, while at the 'lower end', beyond the screens passage, were the service rooms, sometimes with a detached kitchen. The north range in the castle (see p. 31) is a classic example, with the hall at first floor level, over an under-croft. Documents and standing examples show that there were halls of various sizes in many parts of the town, often as part of larger complexes. In 1342 the Abbot of Wigmore sued his tenant, John Hopkins, for demolishing buildings on the north side of Castle Street, with the hall worth £10 and six other rooms together worth £5. Where frontages were long enough, all three parts of a medieval house could face the street. The Rectory, on a five perch wide site, has an undercroft and first floor hall, with a roof that has been dated 1311-28, while a cross wing has evidence of a large original entrance of the same date.

In the late 14th century it was probably Sir Hugh Cheney (d.1404) of Cheney Longville, five times M.P. for Shropshire, who built a stone hall in Mill Street, with service rooms at the lower end and a solar at the upper end, as allowed by a street frontage of six perches. This later became the grammar school. Where sites were narrower, the plan had to be modified, as at 'the House with the Leaden Porch' of the rich Parys family in Castle Street (later Nos.16-18), which had a three perch frontage. Here later buildings represented in fossilised form a recessed hall range and a protruding solar cross wing, with evidence of a detached kitchen at the rear. On two perch wide burgages there was often recourse to a back range at right angles to the street, behind a front unit with its roof line parallel to the street. Most of these front units have been replaced, but a fragment survives at the Bull Hotel and there are several back ranges, as at 10 Broad Street, on the south side of the Angel Yard, and behind 4 Old Street, where the owner was John Hosier, a rich mid-15th century draper.

This picture of Ludlow Grammar School, dating from 1800, shows one of Ludlow's most complete medieval houses before alterations were made in 1802. From left to right:
1: The solar cross-wing, converted to the Headmaster's house after 1527.
2: The hall, lit by two pairs of narrow windows.
3: The arched entrance, leading into the screens passage at the lower end of the hall.
4: The service end, lit by a replacement rectangular window.
The dormer windows were inserted in 1686, when the roof was raised for dormitories.

Left is a picture of Sir Hugh Cheney, taken from a 1663 description of a window in St Laurence's by Elias Ashmole, Windsor Herald.

Knowledge of halls in Ludlow has been greatly enhanced by archaeological excavation on part of the site of the Carmelite Friary in Corve Street, carried out in 1983-85 by a Field Unit from Birmingham University, supported by Ludlow Historical Research Group. Evidence of three successive houses was revealed, all pre-dating the endowment of the Friary in 1350. The lowest levels excavated, from the 12th and 13th centuries, showed first a line of post-holes which marked the back wall of a timber-framed house fronting Corve Street; and then a range of features which were the basis for postulating a small aisled hall, with a service room below the cross passage.

In the late 13th or early 14th centuries this was succeeded by a larger, well-constructed town-house, of at least three rooms. This belonged to Sir Laurence de Ludlow of Stokesay Castle, grandson of the great wool merchant and founder of the Carmelite Friary. Here there was an elaborate floor of glazed tiles, round a rectangular, tiled central hearth. Both of these had impressed themselves in the mortar base, so that the pattern of the floor survived after the tiles had been removed. There were once some 5,500 glazed tiles, many of them highly decorated and in two colours. Ironically, it is likely that about a third of these survive at Stokesay Castle, where they were re-laid in the North Tower in the 19th century, but over a thousand fragments, and 27 complete tiles, were recovered on the Carmelite site, some of them with designs of eagle, an archer, a fish and Fleurs de Lys. They are a splendid indication of the artistry used in one of Ludlow's grander 14th century houses.

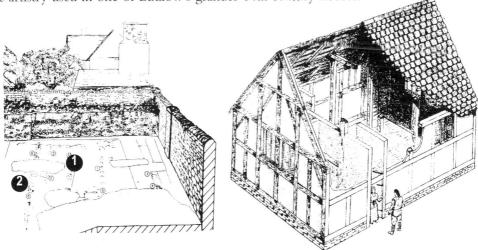

This is a tentative reconstruction of the aisled hall building. It was at least 15 metres wide, facing onto Corve Street. A row of shallow pits filled with stone slabs were interpreted as the bases for internal posts (1) while two deep, square stone-lined post holes showed the position of the doorway (2).

Shops and cellars

Small shops used for manufacture as well as for retailing were numerous in medieval Ludlow, most of them sited along the axial market place. The shops were often eleven feet wide, that is two-thirds of a perch, and the survival of many units of this size, e.g. 2 and 14 High Street and 7, 8 and 13 King Street, is one of the historic features of the Ludlow townscape. They began as stalls, usually in rows, either free standing, as on either side of High Street, or abutting onto pre-existing walls and buildings, as in Drapers' Row, now King Street. At first the shops were lock-up units, with the shop-keepers living elsewhere. Later, cellars were excavated below, for storage, service and other purposes, and solars were erected above for residential use.

Shops were often absorbed into larger building blocks, the first known instance being on the Butter Cross site. In rentals of c.1270 and 1284 'shops belonging to the Palmers' were listed, one having belonged to Geoffrey Andrew; but before 1290 a complex of shops with solars had been built, and was leased to John le Espicer at 32s a year, more than twice the earlier rent of the shops. On the north side of Drapers Row there was a line of eight shops known as 'Taylorsrowe', built against the churchyard. The western two became a property later described as 'a corner house with two shops', while the eastern five, between 1351 and 1436, were embraced into a capital mansion, with 'solars, chambers and kitchens', which became the residence of William Mershetone, a rich burgess. This was one of several properties left to the Guild by Mershetone, their first tenant being Richard Kingston, a land-owner from Ditton Priors who was important enough for this property to be later referred to as 'Kingston's Place'. Another shop and solar complex was at the corner of Old Street and Tower Street. This had four 'shops with solars over', and 'a corner shop with solar over and cellar under'.

Cellars were often leased separately from the rest of the building and were probably undercrofts with direct access from the street, or from a range built later and encroaching onto the street, as at No. 15 King Street. Some cellars were used for selling ale, though the best known building for this purpose was a demesne property on the corner of Broad Street and what is now Market Street, described in the rentals simply as 'The Tavern'.

Kingston Place in the early 1880s, looking east towards the Bull Ring. In 1884 the three furthest shops were replaced by the premises of Gaius Smith, Grocer, but the two on the left are still in use today.

The details of two misericords from the choir stalls of St Laurence's Parish Church, carved in the first half of the 15th century. Copied from pattern books, they illustrate medieval tavern life. Above: a celebration, perhaps even a worshipping, of a wine barrel, while the pots, jugs and barrels are shown in detail. Right: a drunken tapster drawing wine from a cask – this scene may well have occurred in Ludlow taverns, but its moral purpose was to show a servant who is abusing his trust.

61

The Charter of King Edward IV, 1461

The year 1461, when the crown was seized by Edward IV, lord of Ludlow by inheritance from the Mortimers, can be regarded as a major event for the town. The long and verbose charter issued late in the year, on 7 December, was ostensibly a reward for 'laudable and gratuitous services' by the burgesses of Ludlow during the recent wars. In fact, many of its 30 clauses are a confirmation of long established customs and privileges, whereas on other key issues - such as the form of future government for the borough - the charter is imprecise, giving scope for future constitutional wrangles. Nevertheless, the charter is greatly esteemed locally, and is still in the possession of Ludlow Town Council, though it rarely emerges from the security of a local bank. Though lawyers might disagree about their validity, parts of the charter have been cited in late twentieth century debates about local government, for example Clause 5, which states unambiguously:

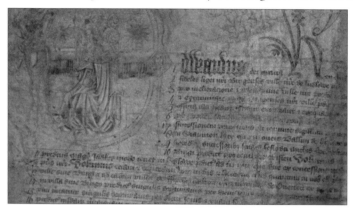

The top left hand corner of the 1461 charter, showing an elaborately decorated E, followed by the letters dwardus. The charter, in Latin, is faded, but a translation was printed by William Felton c 1820

> Also we have granted to our same burgesses, that they, their heirs and successors for ever, shall have one market in the town or borough aforesaid ...

The Charter did allow the burgesses to benefit from the burgage rents and tolls which had previously gone to the lord of the castle, though a yearly fee of £24 3s 4d had to be paid to the Crown for the right to collect rents. The Borough's independence from the County authorities was confirmed, but the most obvious benefit was the right to send two representatives to Parliament, a privilege then held in Shropshire only by Shrewsbury and Bridgnorth. The likelihood of Ludlow members supporting the Yorkists in Parliament was probably, indeed, the fundamental reason why the charter was granted.

CHAPTER FIVE

1461–1642: 'THE LOST CAPITAL OF WALES'

The Council in the Marches

The phrase, The Lost Capital of Wales, coined in 1971 by the Welsh historian A.H. Dodd, catches the special flavour of Ludlow - its *genius loci* - during this period. When Edward IV, heir of the Mortimers, was crowned in 1461, Ludlow became a royal castle, and it was to Ludlow in the early 1470s that he sent his sons Edward and Richard, far away from the plagues and politics of London. The attendant courtiers formed a 'Prince's Council' which undertook some local administration, and though this was discontinued in 1483, after the young princes had left to meet their death in London,

it was later revived by Henry VII. Under the Tudors, with the Council of the North at York and the short-lived Council of the West at Exeter, the Council in the Marches was part of 'the remarkable Tudor policy of creating centralised regional government within England and Wales'. It governed Wales and the border counties, and criminal, civil and ecclesiastical cases were heard in its courts. The Council had several meeting places, including Bewdley, Shrewsbury and Worcester, but its headquarters were at Ludlow. The addition of such an administrative role to the traditional functions of commerce, manufacturing and service was most unusual in a town of Ludlow's size - and had great consequences for Ludlow's social and architectural character.

Mary I, 1516–58, painted after her teenage years in Ludlow.

In the early days royal offspring were sent to reside at Ludlow castle. In January 1501 Prince Arthur, eldest son of Henry VII, came with his bride, Catherine of Aragon. He died on 2 April and his heart was buried in the chancel of St Laurence's, though his body was taken to Worcester where a sumptuous chantry chapel was built. Catherine later married Arthur's brother, who became Henry VIII, and they sent their eldest daughter Mary to Ludlow, where she wintered from 1525 to 1528. The quality of castle life is glimpsed from the will of her Treasurer, Peter Burnell, made in January 1528, which refers to her Chancellor, Dr Denton, and to the clerks of her spicery and her 'Juell House'.

The Council was headed by a Lord President, usually an Englishman. The early Presidents were all bishops, who spent most of their time elsewhere, but in 1534 the Council's authority was increased by Rowland Lee, Bishop of Coventry, who 'made all Wales quake with fear'. Most later presidents were courtiers, one of whom, Lord Zouch, complained in 1602 that he had been sent to a place 'where he desires not to settle'. The longest serving president was Sir Henry Sidney, from 1559 to 1586, but for much of that time he was also Lord Deputy of Ireland. He was succeeded by his son-in-law, the second Earl of Pembroke, descended from the Monmouthshire Herberts.

John Alcock of Hull (d.1500), a 'professional administrator' who was successively Bishop of Rochester, Worcester and Ely; first President of the Council of the Marches, 1473-83.

The Council consisted of all Welsh bishops and judges and a number of lawyers and land-owning gentry. Of 95 laymen appointed under Queen Elizabeth, 55 were from the English border counties - 21 from Shropshire - compared with 23 from other parts of England but only 17 from Wales itself. The whole Council met infrequently, most business being delegated to a smaller group, including a senior judge resident in Ludlow. The Council and its courts were served by a number of salaried officers, the most powerful of whom was Charles Foxe (d.1590), 'a gifted pluralist' who was Secretary of the Council from 1558 and holder of other profitable offices. Another prominent group were the attorneys, so numerous by 1587 that their number was limited to 18, each with one or two clerks. Business dealt with was considerable, records from the 1630s showing that about 1,500 cases were heard a year, the courts sitting during the law terms of Hilary, Lent, Trinity and Michaelmas. Debts and affrays were the most common suits, but critics of the Council alleged that time was wasted on 'trifling and frivolous' matters.

Much building work was carried out at the castle during this period, including 'great raparacions' by Bishop Lee in 1537, using timber from 'an old

Sir Marmaduke Lloyd (1585-1651), Maesyfelin, Cardiganshire. He was the King's Attorney of the Council of the Marches, 1614-22, Puisine Justice of Chester 1622-36, and Chief Justice of Brecknock, 1636-45.

Above: The Judges' Lodgings photographed from the Inner Bailey by Francis Bedford in the 1860s. The Lodgings were a three-storey apartment block of heated chambers, with a polygonal staircase to each floor. Right: Judges' lodgings from the outer bailey sketched by William Stukeley in 1721. The gables and brick chimney stacks are in place.

frerehouse' in the town. There were adaptations to meet the administrative needs of the Council, such as the conversion of St Peter's Chapel into 'a corte house and twoe offices for Recordes', and the provision of more residential accommodation, such as 'the Judges' Lodgings' built by Sir Henry Sidney in the 1580s. Other alterations were in line with the 'great rebuilding' of the time, aiming to provide the amenities to which the upper classes now aspired. In 1580 a new 'chimney of stone' replaced the open hearth in the Great Hall, 'for the safety of the castle ... as also for the better avoiding of smoke ...' A letter of 1634 shows that many rooms had wall hangings, including the chamber 'where the Cheef Justic now lys'. Other rooms were wainscotted while the Great Hall, where banquets and entertainments were held, was richly coloured with shields of former Presidents and Councillors. Leisure was provided for, including an indoor tennis court built by Sir Henry Sidney, while a formal garden and a bowling green were added later. The new style of worship was apparent at St Mary's Chapel, where the chancel was rebuilt and a gallery inserted in the round nave, with covered access from the Great Chamber block.

In 1551 it was claimed that the business of the Council brought to Ludlow 'great accessse of straungers out of all the principality of Wales and the Marches'. The town's inns thrived, especially The Crown and The Angel, which faced each other across Broad Street. In 1587 the poet Thomas Churchyard noted:

> The houses such, where straungers lodge at will,
> As long as there the council lists abide

Records testify to the number of long-term lodgers in the town, e.g. the will of Ann Cother, widow, made in 1613, which refers to a room in her house as 'Mr John Pearce's chamber'; while in 1629 Mr Phillips, clerk, had a chamber in the Bull Ring house of Mr Justice Waties.

The Council brought custom to local traders, such as the 'sweet water and damaske powder to perfume the rooms of my lord's lady coming from London', bought from Winwood the apothecary in 1615. A list of persons receiving salaries from the Council in 1603 includes a number of Ludlow residents, among them Elizabeth Butler, widow, paid £8 8s 'for washing linen'. Affluent Council members and officers were able to buy luxury items from the town's mercers, for example Sir Charles Foxe of Bromfield, who on 23 September 1617 paid £4 17s 6d to Valentine Dawes, who had a large shop and house at what is now 10 Church Street for 4 yeardes qu(a)rter & haulf qu(a)rter of silke Russet Cloth with silke velvet & lace to furnishe me a Cloke. Some items, however, had to come from outside the town, such as the 'two new close stools' bought at Worcester in 1615.

There was some social interaction with the town, as in 1536, 'when ye counsyle dynyd wt ye lords in ye christmas'. The town had a long tradition of professional entertainment - 6s 8d was paid to 'the kinges Mynstrell' in 1466-67 - but some events were staged in association with the Council, as in 1576-77, when 13s 4d were 'geven to my lorde stafordes players in the ester weeke that played in the castell'. The town's deference to the Council is indicated by the appointment of a committee of Councillors in 1581-82 'to conferre ... how my L(o)rd president shall be gratified by ye Town towards ye keepinge of St Georges his day'. In the 1590s the Christmas courts of the Earl of Pembroke were 'brilliant social occasions', where, according to a contemporary, a young man might learn 'good behaviour and manners ... among such honourable, worshipfull and gentlemanlie companie'.

One festivity at the castle was that of Michaelmas day, 1634, when a masque, written by the young poet John Milton, was performed to mark the first visit to the

POEMS
OF
Mr. *John Milton*,
BOTH
ENGLISH and LATIN,
Compos'd at feveral times.

Printed by his true Copies.

The S O N G S were fet in Mufick by
Mr. H E N R Y L A W E S Gentleman of
the K I N G S Chappel, and one
of His M A I E S T I E S
Private Mufick.

—— Baccare frontem
Cingite, ne vati noceat mala lingua futuro,
Virgil, Eclog. 7.

Printed and publifh'd according to
O R D E R.

LONDON,
Printed by *Ruth Raworth* for *Humphrey Mofeley*,
and are to be fold at the figne of the Princes
Arms in S. *Pauls* Church-yard. 1645.

A
M A S K
Of the fame
AUTHOR
P·R·E·S·E·N·T·E·D
At *L U D L O W*-Caftle,
1 6 3 4.

Before
The Earl of B R I D G E W A T E R
Then Prefident of W A L E S.

Anno Dom. 1 6 4 5.

The frontispiece and title page of the 1645 edition of the poems of John Milton (1608-74). This edition contained most of his shorter poems, though his major works, Paradise Lost and Paradise Regained, were written many years later. Each poem in the 1645 edition has its own title page, that for the masque later known as Comus being shown on the right.

Marches of the Earl of Bridgwater, Lord President since 1631. It was attended by 'a large concourse of nobility and gentry' but it was also 'a joyeous family occasion', with three of the Earl's 15 children taking part, while the Attendant Spirit was Henry Lawes, their music tutor. The masque became popular in the 18th century, when it was called Comus after the principal character, though 'A Masque presented at Ludlow' was retained as a sub-title. As appreciation of Milton's poetry grew, many visitors noted Ludlow's association with Comus, one of them writing in 1813:

> Here Milton sang. What needs a greater spell
> To lure thee stranger to these far-famed walls?

The town showed deference to the Council in a number of other ways. Gifts were regularly given to Council members and officials, as in 1556-57, when the Bailiffs' Accounts included 'a hogsheade of wyne for the counseyll at Xmas'. Arrangements were sometimes made to entertain society from the castle, as in 1625-26, when the bailiffs: payd for a carte to carry chayres and Stoales into the ould fyld [now the Race Course] when the Traynings [the Trained Bands] were here for the Countess and other gentlewomen

Church bells were rung when Council dignitaries entered or left the town, as in 1616, when 2s were paid to the ringers 'for cominge in of my lord president gerrard'. Pews for the Council and their Ladies were provided in the parish church, and entries in the Church Wardens Accounts show these were kept in good repair, as in 1607-08, when 9s 4d was paid to William Hill mercer 'for green bayis for the pewe of Ladye Lucknor', wife of the Chief Justice. Sir Henry Sidney, in particular, took a personal interest in music at St Laurence's, which during his presidency had a paid musical establishment of organist, six men and six boys, a complement which has been rated as 'slightly fewer than in most cathedrals but considerably higher than those in other parish church choirs'. A number of impressive public ceremonies were held, involving church, castle and proclamations at the High Cross, while the elaborate tombs in St Laurence's, beginning with that of fourteen year old Ambrosia Sidney, who died in 1574, are a continuing reminder of the Council's presence in Ludlow.

The effigy of Dame Mary Eure, who died 19 March, 1612, aged 55. She was the wife of Lord Ralph Eure, Baron of Malton, Lord President of the Council of the Marches, 1607-1616. There are several references to Lady Eure in the Church Wardens' Accounts, e.g. in 1609: to John havorde....for a walenut boorde to make the desk in my laddy Ewers pewe & a planke to enlarge the dore of the same pewe.

Population and Plague

The study of urban populations at this time presents many problems and tentative estimates are the best that can be hoped for. For Ludlow, as for other towns, a survey of chantry endowments in 1545 gives the number of 'housling people' - communicants probably aged twelve years or older - as 1800, which, it has been suggested, gives an estimated population of about 2,500. This is well below estimates which have been made for regional centres such as Bristol (10,000) or the larger county towns such as Worcester (4,250), but puts Ludlow at the top end of the seven or eight hundred small or medium sized towns which bespattered the country at this time. It was larger, for instance, than Leominster, which had 1700 'housling people', though perhaps a quarter of these lived in the extensive rural parts of that parish; and considerably larger than towns such as Bromyard and Ledbury.

The estimate for Ludlow is not inconsistent with the town's known importance in the late medieval period and with its developing role as a centre of regional administration. In 1535, however, Ludlow was one of a group of towns, including Bridgnorth, Northampton, Nottingham and Shrewsbury, listed in 'an Acte for reedyfyeng of dyv(er)s Townes in the Realme', and this was repeated, with many other towns added, in 1543. A 1525 Rental of the Palmers' Guild, which describes some Ludlow properties as decayed and reduces the rents of others, confirms this picture of urban malaise, while a schedule of the Guild estate in 1551, listing 172 properties, describes 31 of them as 'greatly in ruins' and eleven as 'totally in decay'. If the proportion of untenanted Guild properties reflects the town as a whole, then Ludlow's population earlier in the 16th century may have been as high as 3,300.

Estimates after 1543 must be even more tentative, though there are some grounds for supposing that population declined into the late 1550s, when a severe influenza epidemic swept the country. The parish registers available from 1558 suggest, however, that the population soon reached the level of the 1540s and may have been as high as 3,000 by the 1580s, a supposition which is supported by the recovery in rent values. There were then a number of fluctuations, with the total in 1641 being about 2,600, as indicated through detailed family reconstructions by Michael Faraday.

As in other towns, epidemics caused sudden fluctuations in the death rate. For the first part of the period these can be charted from probate records, which reveal years with many deaths, including 1509, in the June of which John Browne had to name a second executor in his will 'foreasmuch as Margery my wife ys sore greved and vexed with infirmitie of Pestilence'. After 1558 the parish registers reveal a large number of burials in some harvest years (August to the following July), including 1586, 1587, 1597, 1608, 1609, 1623 and 1635. Some of these were due to successive poor harvests, as in 1597, at the end of four poor years. Others, however, were due to the dreaded plague, including that of 1608 and 1609, when 104 who died in this way are marked in the register. The plague struck several members of some families, beginning with the Dericots, but the most afflicted were the Shrawleys, seven of whom died within 19 days: Richard Shrawley, clothier, his wife Joan, three of their four young children, and Richard's brother Thomas and his wife Mary. Desperate measures were taken to prevent or limit the plague, including a ban on London carriers and the building or adoption of 'pest houses', one of these being situated 'a bow shot from the town'.

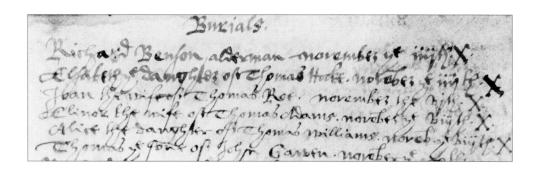

Richard Benson alderman november ye iiijth X
Elizabeth ye daughter of Thomas Hooke. november ye iiijth X
Joan the wife of Thomas Roe. november the vjth X
Elinor the wife of Thomas Adams nove(m)ber the viijth X
Alice the daughter of Thomas Williams nove(m)b(er) ye viijth X
Thomas ye sone of John Gawen nove(m)ber ye xth

Burials recorded in the register of St Laurence's parish church for November, 1609. The X at the end of the first five entries indicates that these persons died of the plague.

Farming and the Town Fields

Like other medieval and early modern towns, Ludlow was close to nature, and the yearly calendar was essentially that of the seasons. The quality of the harvest affected many aspects of life, as noted by President Bishop Lee in 1534, when he wrote to Thomas Cromwell that: The scarceness of grain arises daily and it causes more roberies. Although items from afar such as salt, garlic and fish were bought at the weekly market or the annual fairs, most of Ludlow's food came from its fields or from the surrounding countryside. A few specialist farmers lived in Ludlow, such as Robert Toy, a Galdeford husbandman, who died in 1498, rich enough to leave his wife jewels as well as corn and hay. Many more people were part-time farmers, who also had another occupation. In 1597, for example, Richard Benson, ironmonger, had hay 'ready to be ynned' in a meadow near what is now Henley Road, where he employed Arthur Haynes, labourer, who 'had a cart to help him'. Some Ludlow burgesses had farming interests further afield, such as Lawrence Beck, weaver, who had 69 cattle, as well as horses and mares, in rural Wales when he died in 1579.

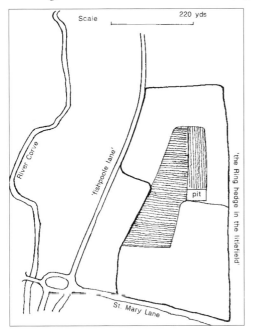

The extent of 'the litefield' in 1562, showing the alignment of ridges in two furlongs. St Mary's Lane is now New Road.

The greater part of the land within the liberties of Ludlow was taken up with food production. Crops were grown in large open fields (see Fig 9). The three in the west formed a group known as 'Halton Fields', while there were five fields in the east, including Hucklemarsh Field, named after the butchery term 'huckle', meaning 'the leg and loin'; and Waretree Field, named after the 'wartree' or gallows which stood at the top of what is now Charlton Rise. Within each field there were long strips or selions, but a survey of 1562 shows that in most cases these had been amalgamated into larger units known as furlongs. Thus in Little Field a 'one aker' furlong had 'vij ridges shoting north and south', while a larger furlong to the west, below what is now Castle View Terrace, had 'liij short ridges shotying est and west', the preference on this steep land being to plough up and down, rather than along the contours.

71

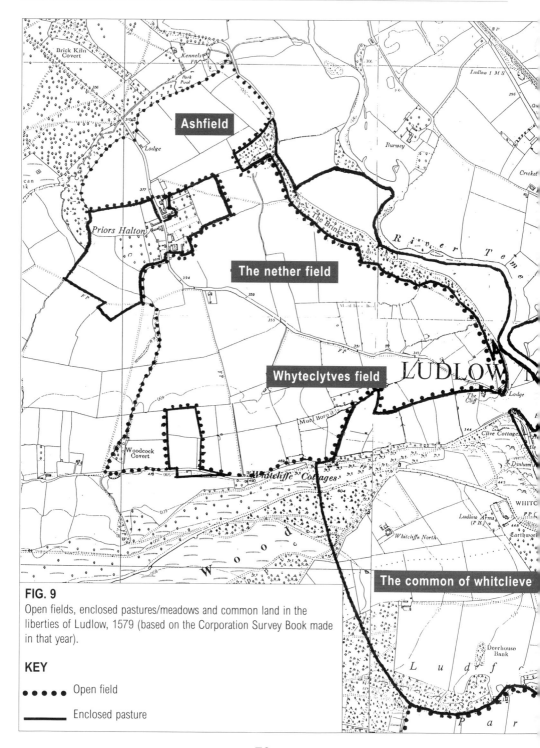

Ashfield

The nether field

Whyteclytves field

The common of whitclieve

FIG. 9

Open fields, enclosed pastures/meadows and common land in the liberties of Ludlow, 1579 (based on the Corporation Survey Book made in that year).

KEY

●●●●● Open field

───── Enclosed pasture

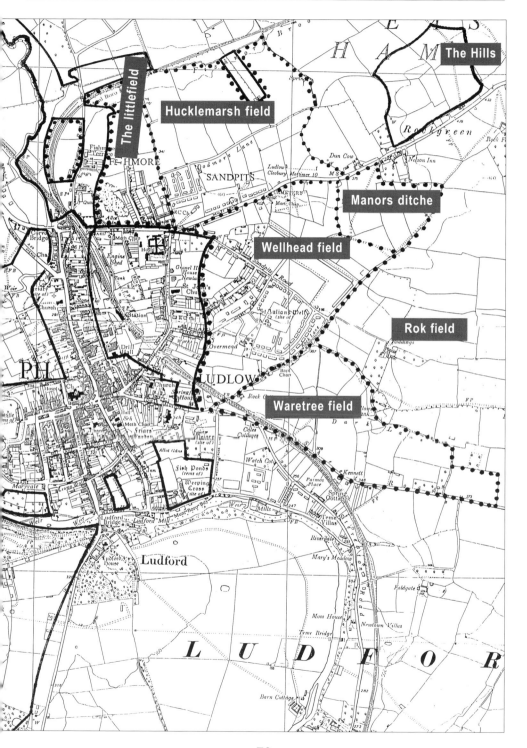

In 1579, and probably at other times, a three-fold rotation was used. Three fields were 'with corne this yere', corn being a mixture of wheat, rye and barley, all of which were mentioned by William Beck, husbandman, when he gave evidence on land use in 1599. Other fields were 'with oates this yere', while the rest were fallow. All the fields were surrounded by ring hedges, to keep out stray beasts, but after 'sickle and sythe', burgesses could graze their animals on the stubble.

As shown on Fig 9, there were closes or pieces of enclosed land between the open fields and the town, most of which were described in 1579 as 'pasture enclosed'. These can be most clearly seen on what is now Gravel Hill, where two of them were each described as 'the brickclose' at various times. There were also several pieces of meadow, as adjoining the River Corve and in Linney, where large crops of hay were produced, and industrial crops such as hemp sometimes grown. Whitcliffe Common, however, remained the largest area of pasture, for cattle, sheep and pigs. In 1577 John Taylor, tanner, and Richard Farr, mercer, were in dispute over 'the confushion of their cattle on Wytcliffe'; in 1590 Thomas Piers was accused of sheep stealing 'on the common'; while in 1629 John Warden was going along Lower Broad Street 'with his master's swine to Whitcliffe'. Orchards and gardens, occupying the rear of burgages, were other important sources of food supply within the borough itself, and fruit are often cited in wills, as in 1590, when William Bedowe left his friend Thomas ap Robert 'one bushel of apples and one hundred of wardens [cooking pears] yearly ... to be taken out of my orchard adjoining to my dwelling house on the west side of Corvestreet'.

This eighteenth century view from near Ludford Bridge shows Whitcliffe Common before parts of it were sold and enclosed in 1793.

Markets and fairs

In the Tudor period, Ludlow was one of some 800 market towns in England and Wales, the survivors of a much larger number which had been active in the Middle Ages. Some of the smaller markets in south Shropshire - Burford, Richard's Castle, Wistanstow - had lapsed, and by 1552 Monday had replaced Thursday as market day at Ludlow, to avoid competition with Knighton and Kidderminster. The May fair, also, had been discontinued by this date, but the traditional fairs of St Laurence (August 10) and St Catherine (November 25) were supplemented in 1596 by a Whitsun fair and in 1604 by a fair at St Lambert (17 September). Markets and fairs were administered by the Corporation, who leased the collection of tolls and took rent from standings. Forestallers (those trading outside the market) were fined at the town courts, as in 1603, when seven women were presented for selling fruit. Burgesses were exempted tolls and stall rents, while outsiders were sometimes actively discouraged, as in 1597 when a Shrewsbury upholsterer was refused permission to trade, after a mob had demolished his stall.

Town court records reveal, however, that traders came considerable distances to Ludlow fairs, especially after 1600. These included a feltmaker from Brecon, a glass-vendor from Bromyard, a button-maker from Worcester, and a cutler from Tutbury. Many buyers, predictably, came from Wales, such as James Owen of Carmarthanshire, Gent., in 1636, while in 1610 Thomas Harrison, a Birmingham butcher, was purchasing livestock. The great majority of those before the court, however, were from Ludlow or the surrounding countryside: people such as Alice, wife of Richard Wood of Eyton, Shropshire, who came to Ludlow with her maid to a January market in 1630 to buy Welsh inkle (thread); or Joseph Harper of Knighton-on-Teme, husbandman, who came in December 1635 to buy salt.

The markets and fairs were held in the streets of Ludlow, especially in or near the historic High Street. The centre of the livestock market was the present Bull Ring, then called 'the beaste market', with the Tolsey or toll house in the middle, but animal standings spread into adjoining streets, especially Old Street and Corve Street. The stench and the squalor can hardly be imagined. Many towns acquired market houses in the mid 16th century, and at Ludlow a single storey building was erected in what is now Castle Square. In 1556-57 the Chamberlain's Accounts show stone being used 'to syll' and pave the market house, while later repairs refer to timber pillars and a shingle roof. The poet Churchyard recorded in 1587 that 'corne and oates' were sold here, but there were other items as well, including brass and pewter ware displayed by Henry Floid of Walsall on 10 August, 1630. Stalls were squeezed in at a number of places, including what is now High Street, where John Bowen of Neen Savage, a petty chapman, had a standing 'to sell some small wares' at St Catherine's Fair, 1629. In 1558 Thomas Cother had a 'stall shoppe or borde' near the Cross, where he sold fish, while by 1592 a new Shambles - two rows of six butchers' shops with lofts above - had been established at the top of Mill Street.

Shopkeepers also did good business on market and fair days. An analysis of debts recorded in wills of Ludlow residents between 1540 and 1630 shows many commercial links with central Wales, part of a process by which the larger border towns carved out a segment of the Welsh upland as their catchment zone. William Adams, cutler, who died in 1560, had creditors at Presteigne and Builth, while Samuel Parker, mercer, who died in 1618, supplied Rees ap David and Margaret his wife of Llandrindod with their wedding apparel. Some shops were still trestle-like stalls, but others had interiors which customers entered, such as the High Street shop of Thomas Jones, mercer, which John Hopkins of Elton 'went into' to buy playing cards and to view a 'belt and girdles upon a chest ... from London'.

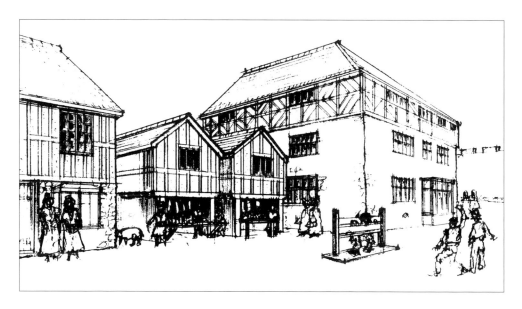

An artist's reconstruction of what the Shambles might have looked like at the top of Mill Street in the early seventeenth century. On the right is Castle Lodge and on the left the White Horse Inn, where the Assembly Rooms are now. The pillory was at the top of Mill Street, facing the Shambles.

Occupations and trade guilds

The occupational structure of a town's workforce is of great interest for urban historians, but firm data is rarely available before the decennial census returns of the 19th century. For most towns, however, estimates can be made from a number of sources, and four sets of figures researched for Ludlow are tabulated below. Each source used has a number of difficulties and two of them - freeman admissions and probates - are biased in favour of the richer citizens. Nevertheless, a basic pattern is discernible, with the cloth trades ranging from 33 to 22%, followed by the leather trades from 24 to 14%. Numbers, of course, are not necessarily commensurate with wealth or influence, and other kinds of figures are needed, e.g. the persons of each occupational group on the Borough Corporation, to assess the role of the mercers or of those in the professions or involved with the Council of the Marches.

FIG.10 Numbers of persons in occupational groups, calculated from four sources

	Freemen admissions 1526-83	Parish Registers 1558-1642	Muster Roll 1614	Probates 1300-1659
Building trades	3	5	13	10
Cloth making	29	26	46	60
Cloth using	19	26	15	19
Council of the Marches	-	13	22	29
Farmer	11	-	8	20
Food and drink	18	23	50	48
Labourers	-	23	5	5
Leather making	21	5	13	15
Leather using	15	23	44	43
Mercers	22	11	21	23
Metal trades	5	11	19	22
Professions	4	22	9	23
Transport	-	2	6	4
Wood trades	-	5	9	9
Total	**147**	**195**	**280**	**330**

The making and selling of cloth was Ludlow's major economic activity, with nearly a third of the freemen being cloth makers, cloth users or mercers. There were signs of decline after 1600 but in 1614 nearly a quarter of the 280 heads of household who paid subsidy were still engaged with cloth. Some of the cloth was sold locally but the tailors and hatters never attained the influence of the manufacturers and merchants. It was the reverse with the leather trades, where a few tanners supplied a large number of shoemakers and some saddlers, with glovers increasing in importance after 1600. The food and drink trades, including innkeeping, accounted for nearly a fifth of those with known occupations in 1614, comparable with figures at larger towns such as Leicester and York, which had, it is claimed, 'broadly based economies with a regional servicing function'. At Ludlow, the building, metal and wood trades accounted for under 15% of the 1614 sample, with the practitioners generally of modest wealth and social standing. Labourers are insignificant in three cases, but account for 12% of the parish register entries – an indication that this group is under-represented in the other lists.

Numbers in each trade in medium sized towns like Ludlow were often small, so the need to have guilds strong enough to support and protect their members was often met by amalgamation. In the 16th century two such guilds were formed in Ludlow: the Hammermen and the Stitchmen. The charter of the Hammermen, granted by the Bailiffs in 1511, list 22 trades, but the 124 recorded admissions between 1534 and 1583 added another four. The largest numbers were carpenters (17), joiners (17), tilers (16) and smiths (15), but there were also nine ironmongers, seven glaziers and six cutlers, though only a singe pewterer and no braziers. Both the later trades, however, were practised in Ludlow after 1590. A rather looser grouping were the Stitchmen, who grew out of what was called in 1542 'the occupation of taylors and mercers', but by the 17th century the membership also included cappers, drapers, glovers and hatters. Some guilds, however, retained a distinct identity, including the butchers, shoemakers and weavers, all of whom had chancels in the parish church where members were sometimes buried. Thus Roger Bebb, butcher, willed in 1610 to be buried 'in the butchers' chancel of St Laurence's parish church', which was in what is now the north transept.

A major role of the Guilds was to regulate entry and to ensure that all practitioners had served an apprenticeship. At best this was a guarantee of good standards, at worst the restrictive control of an oligarchy. Of 36 admissions to the Stitchmen in the early 1600s, 17 had served apprenticeships in Ludlow, three of them with their own fathers. The rest had served apprenticeships elsewhere, twelve of them in London. In contrast, some sons of Ludlow burgesses served apprenticeships and set up businesses in other places, e.g. Richard Dodmore who was apprenticed in the 1520s to Walter Dodmore his uncle, a City of London merchant tailor. In 1540 he had his shop in Watling Street! The registers of the London Stationers record seven Ludlow boys apprenticed in London between 1564 and 1597 while the Calendar of Bristol Apprentices, 1542-1552, records three Ludlow boys in Bristol, apprenticed to a merchant, a grocer and a draper.

The Ludlow guilds took proceedings against tradesmen who were not properly admitted, as in 1617, when William Lane was presented to the Town Court 'for pursuing the trade of a tailor within this town, being not free of the same'. The guilds also cared for members in difficulty, as in 1609, when the Stitchmen voted 3s 4d to Ryes ap Powell, 'a decayed brother of this company'. Each guild was administered by small groups of elected officials, many of whom held other posts in the town. In 1603 the 'Six Men' of the Hammermen included two ironmongers who were Corporation members: Robert Sanders and Richard Benson, both of whom served as High Bailiff. The Hammermen met in the south aisle of St Laurence's, where their 1514 charter obliged them 'to keep a light there in the chancel of St Loye'. After the Reformation they had five pews where that chancel had been in the south aisle, but there was often over-crowding, especially from journeymen, apprentices and widows, and in 1625 five more pews were taken in the new south gallery. Members who missed meetings paid a fine in wax for candles. A more serious offence was poaching work, which brought a 3s 4d fine, as did 'using rayling words'.

The 'great box' and the 'comon box' of the Stitchmen. Documents were kept in the 'great box' and money in the 'comon box'. Both were in the custody of the Six Men, who appointed key-keepers annually.

Cloth manufacture and distribution

Cloth manufacture usually had specialist craftsmen engaged on one or more processes. These were often organised by clothiers, who infused capital where it was needed and made large profits by selling the finished cloth. The finished cloth was tested for quality by the aulnager, and at Ludlow a series of accounts shows that most cloth was presented by clothiers, though some also came from weavers, drapers and mercers.

Carding – disentangling the fibres – and spinning were largely done on a domestic basis. Many wills refer to small stocks of wool, e.g. Gillian Blunt (d.1624), spinster, had 5 lbs of coarse wool, while Thomas Bowdler (d.1606), clothier, who occupied Kingston Place in Drapers' Row, left 'to every of my spinners 4d.' The weavers were a large group, many of local importance, such as Richard Downe (d.1531), Warden of the Palmers' Guild. Several weavers had a broad loom and a narrow loom and sometimes additional details are given, as by Thomas Bordell (d.1549), who had 'hooks, stays and shuttles'. The woven cloth went through finishing processes, including fulling, dyeing and shearing. Some tradesmen undertook more than one process, as is clear from the will of John Bowdler (d.1590), who had a 'hole furnace' for dyeing and 'two pairs of shearman's shears', though his main trade was that of a walker or fuller. Dyeing needed much equipment, including a large furnace, that of Edward Amyas in 1622 having a fire hole underneath large enough 'for a vagrant to sleep in'. The cloth was then cropped or sheared and the final stage was tentering, when it was stretched on racks to which it was attached by tenter hooks. The accounts of Sir Charles Foxe of Bromfield, kept intermittently from 1593 to 1630, give a glimpse of how Ludlow textile workers had custom from a local landowner. In six years, Foxe placed 50 orders with weavers, 24 with dyers, and 28

This detail from a 1826 painting by Henry Ziegler shows the fulling mill at the bottom of Lower Broad Street. Fulling was the closing of the fibres to thicken the cloth, a process powered by water-driven hammers. Tenters' racks, attached to Ludlow's only surviving cloth manufactory, can be seen on the left.

for 'walking and dressing'. For weaving, 11 craftsmen were used, most orders being for hemp or flax, but there are references to medley cloth, petticoat cloth and blankets. Orders to dyers were mostly for cloth for clothes, as in 1620, when 'gode weffe amias' was paid 8s for 'colouring xij yardes of Cloth to make a suit' for Foxe's son Roger. In his later years when Ludlow cloth-making was declining, Sir Charles bought much of his better cloth elsewhere, as in 1623, when he paid a London tailor £10 5s 'for 27 yardes of Cloth for my servants liveries'.

For the 55 years for which aulnager's accounts are available from 1475 to 1610, the number of cloths averaged 466, but the range of annual totals was wide, with nine of more than 600 cloths and ten below 300, though most of the latter were after 1595. The most productive decade was in the 1580's, when seven yearly totals give an average of 634 cloths. For 25 of the 55 years, the names of the producers are given, but nearly two thirds of the total came from 18 producers, and nearly a quarter from one family, the Blashfields. Most of the bigger producers were styled 'clothiers' and operated from the town centre, including Thomas Blashfield from 1-2 Market Street, and the Hooke family from 16-18 Castle Street, then called 'The house with the Leaden Porch'. Others were clustered round the Bull Ring or on the east side of Corve Street, while Richard Rascoll (d.1611), the largest producer after the Blashfields, was at 54 Old Street. These clothiers were an influential group in the town, 11 of them being members of the Corporation, and 14 serving as church warden. But many people produced only a few cloths, e.g. Laurence Beck, weaver, who presented just 25 cloths in the 1550s.

No references have been found in the Tudor era to the brightly coloured cloths exported by Ludlow clothiers in the Middle Ages. In 1590, however, 'five coarse cloths called Ludlow Whytes' worth £17 10s were on sale in London, while there is a reference in 1601 to 'two broadcloths containing 30 yards apiece of white woollen brodecloth'. These were probably low-quality cloths woven from short stapled wool and thickly fulled to give a felt-like finish. This kind of cloth had dominated the English cloth industry for much of the Middle Ages, even though high quality worsteds, made from fine long fibres, were of increasing importance in East Anglia and other favoured localities.

Competition from such 'New Draperies' is probably a reason why cloth manufacture declined at Ludlow and a number of other centres. The sharp drop in the number of cloths sealed by the aulnager after 1600, with no entries at all after 1610, pin-points this decline, and is supported by the conversion of mills from fulling to grinding corn, and by the decreasing number of cloth manufacturers on the Corporation. It has been suggested above that about a sixth of the labour force was still engaged with cloth in 1614, but this may have been largely for a local market, where the aulnager's seal was not required. A local factor might have been a tendency by some manufacturers to aspire too readily to the status and way of life of the grandees in the castle. Thomas Blashfield junior, for instance, after his father's death in 1593, built himself a new house at 'The Friars' in Corve Street, and also accepted office as Sergeant at Mace to the Council of the Marches. The symbol of this office and the initials T.B. still proudly decorate the arch of his house, moved in the 19th century to the Linney entrance to St Leonard's churchyard, a hint, perhaps, that his aspirations were rather different from his father's.

The yard behind Nos.1–2 Market Street, the house and commercial premises of Thomas Blashfield senior (d.1593), as sketched by Joy Wheeler-Phillips in 1996. The premises were later The Red Lion Inn.

The archway into the new house of Thomas Blashfield junior (d.1598), drawn in its original position in Corve Street. The drawing was made in the 1830s by the Shropshire antiquarian Thomas Farmer Dukes.

Faith and worship

Before the Reformation Ludlow people retained well established beliefs and continued to use the town's endowed institutions for salvation. Many wills began with dedications such as that of Nicholas Cresset, who in 1481 gave his soul to 'Almighty God and lady saint Mary and all the holy company of heaven'. Wealthy people requested elaborate funerals, as did Katrine Wollastoll in 1530:

I will that the parson with all the priests of the Guild and all other prests within the town be at my dirge and masses and all the two orders of frers

A number of new chantry chapels were founded in the parish church, among them that for Piers Beaupie, cofferer to Edward IV and M.P. for Ludlow. Beaupie's bequests to the church - vestments of silk and camlet, a new Missal, a large breviary, an image of Jesus Christ, 'another Image after the likeness of God sitting upon a Throne with the four evangelists', two candelabra of gold - is just one of a number of glimpses of the colour and ritual of worship at this time. Another comes from the inventory taken at the Carmelite Friary in 1538, which includes 'a fair mass book, written', a 'sacring bell' and an image of Our Lady of Pity holding the reserved sacrament. The fine series of Church Wardens Accounts which begin in 1540 add further details on ritual, such as payment 'to weeche [watch] the sepulcre' from Good Friday to Easter.

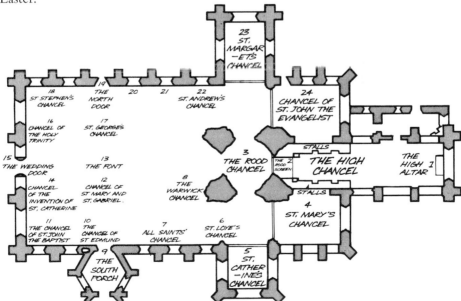

FIG.11 The location of chantry chapels in St Laurence's in the early 16th century. Chantries were substantial structures, often enclosed by open screen work, with an altar and reredos at the east end. Images, tabernacles and 'voltes' [vaults] were sold by the Church Wardens as the chantries were demolished in the late 1540s.

As elsewhere, scandals afflicted Ludlow's religious houses especially St John's Hospital, where the Prior, John Holland, was accused of incontinence with three local women in 1501, two of them married. Numbers at the Friaries were very low by the 1530s, but both the Austin and Carmelite Friars attracted some gifts, while in 1538 it was said that 'The friars in these parts ... have many favourers, and great labour is made for their continuance'. In terms of communal support, however, the most successful institution was the Palmers' Guild, a well established body which could offer the benefit of chaplains saying prayers on behalf of members, before and after death. Membership was expensive, so the Guild was a middle and upper class institution, with many gentry, clergy and merchants. In the early 16th century enrolment was huge, with members living as far away as London, Lincoln and Manchester, but there was some decline in the 1530s, as Protestantism spread and as the Guild's future seemed less secure. The guild's social responsibilities included the grammar school, which moved to the 'voyde Great House' in Mill Street in 1527, and the almshouses endowed by John Hosier, a rich draper who died in 1463. The Guild chaplains helped to maintain the daily round of masses and obits in the parish church, and maintained the organist and 'singing-men'. By purchase and endowment the Guild increased its real estate, owning some 230 properties in Ludlow by 1546 and several others outside the town.

| | Richard davies for rent of a shoppe by ther | iiijs |
| altz xvjd | Thom(a)s gossenyll now Roger fferne for rent of a shoppe w(i)t(h) a soller by yere | xiij iiijd |

A small part of the Palmers' Guild rental for 1525, listing properties on the north side of what is now High Street. The upper entry, relating to what is now 2 High Street, describes a single storey shop, but the next property, now 3 High Street, had a solar or living room above. The marginal note shows that 3 High Street was one of many properties with a reduced rent at this time.

84

The two friaries and St John's Hospital surrendered their estates to the King's commissioners in 1538. The Austin Friary buildings were converted into a mansion for Sir Robert Townsend, Chief Justice of Chester, while part of the Hospital was turned into an additional house for the Foxes of Ludford – and remains as one of the town's best preserved Tudor houses. The Carmelite site was acquired by Thomas Vernon of Stokesay Castle, but was much fragmented before part of it was used by Thomas Blashfield junior as described above. The Palmers Guild survived longer, but was dissolved as a result of the Chantries Acts of 1545 and 1547. As in many other towns, however, their estates were formally ceded to the Borough in 1552, which assumed many Guild responsibilities. These included maintenance of the grammar school and the almshouses, as well as the provision of a Preacher and a Reader at St Laurence's, and the payment of an organist and choristers.

An incident in 1529, when Henry Clee was accused of saying, 'in the presence of many people', that 'hytt was not the good lorde that the preeste dyd heve over hys hedd at masses', is an indication that the doctrinal debates of the day had an echo at Ludlow. Perplexity was perhaps the response of the Warden of the Palmers' Guild, Walter Rogers, for the preamble to his will, made in 1546, refers to 'temptations laid against me ... by problems of brain or other occasion'. Less thoughtful Ludlow residents would certainly have been amazed at the changes to St Laurence's, as 'the rood and images' were taken down in 1548, as box pews were built, as the walls were whittened, and as the English prayer book replaced 'the old bookes of the old service' which were sold for 2s 8d. There were some reversals during the reign of Queen Mary (1553-58), but as early as 1555 Peter Ford, tailor, had a preamble to his will in which he trusted 'by the meryts of Christs passion' to be one of the 'elect number in the Kingdom of Heaven'.

By the 1560s the new Protestant order was well established, with regular services as described by Thomas Churchyard:

> Three times a day in church good service is
> At six o'clock, at nine and then at three
> At which due howers, a stranger shall not mis,
> But sondrie sorts of people there to see

Pews were leased, as in 1570, when 'one pewe next unto the churche wedding doere' went to Walter Langford, landlord of The Angel, for iiijs, while lawyer Mr Edmunde Walter paid vs. for one pew 'on the southe syde by the pyller downewards, next unto the clock'. In the early 17th centuries galleries were built at the west end and over the north and south aisles, the latter being 'The Scholars Gallery', given by Margaret Greene, a 'vertous maiden'. Preaching was central to worship, but the only surviving sermons are those of Robert Horne, Rector 1596-1604, which are of prodigious length. An example is that on The Shield of the Righteous or the Ninety first Psalm', where 36 doctrines are expounded, one being 'As men offend early or late, night or day, God hath plagues ready to send upon them at all hours'.

The religious controversies of the time had their impact on Ludlow, though

A Puritan at prayer: Sir John Walter (1566-1630), a weeper on the tomb of his parents. He had a distinguished legal career, becoming Baron of the Exchequer, though he later lost the favour of Charles I because of his constitutional views.

they apparently did not arouse great passion. A few recusants were regularly presented for non-attendance, the most prominent being the Townsend family, who were still influential enough to locate the grand tomb of Sir Robert Townsend in the sanctuary in 1580. There was a sizeable Puritan faction , encouraged by some local gentry, especially the Harleys of Brampton Bryan. Robert Horne had Puritan inclinations, being presented in 1601 for 'Not wearing a surplis' and for allowing communicants 'to stand and sit'. He resigned in 1604 but remained active in the district under the patronage of the Walters of Richard's Castle, where he had the title of Preacher. As before the Reformation, many people were presented for sexual offences, e.g. Brigit Whinne in 1597 'for being a lewd liver'; but few could emulate John Lloyd, thatcher, presented by his wife in 1621 for 'lieing with his cozen Alice Nixon in bed between his wife and her'. There were also periodic but not totally successful drives to enforce sabbath observance, as in 1618, when John Probert was 'playing the tables during divine service'.

The Twelve and Twenty Five

Like most corporate towns, Ludlow had a two-tier system of oligarchic rule. There were 12 Aldermen - a historian of Lincoln has called the Aldermen there 'a civic aristocracy' - and 25 Common Councillors. These constituted the Borough Corporation, which was self-electing, with nearly all members remaining in office for life. When there was a vacancy, the members chose a successor: from the 25 if an Alderman had died, and to the 25 from the burgesses or commonalty. Members came from the upper echelons of Ludlow society, and were often related to each other, especially those who achieved the highest offices. Of 195 Corporation members whose occupations are known, the two largest groups were cloth makers and users (27%) and merchants or mercers (23%). Many came from the leather trades, especially after 1600, and from food and drink trades, especially innkeepers, but only 13 were associated with the Council of the Marches and there were just eight from the professions.

The civic year began on 28 October, the Festival of St Simon and St Jude, when two bailiffs were chosen as the Borough's chief officers: a High Bailiff from the 12, a Low Bailiff from the 25. They were assisted by a chamberlain, a coroner and an aulnager, all elected from the 25. Most Corporation members also served for a year as church warden, usually before election to the 25, and all had to have the status of burgess - achievable by being the son of a burgess, by marrying a burgess's daughter or by becoming a freeman of one of the town's trades.

These offices provided a career structure for men who sought status and influence in the Borough. Only just over a third of those whose careers can be traced became High Bailiff, but several persons held that office three or more times, among them Walter Rogers (d.1546), his son-in-law Richard Langford (d.1563), and Richard's father, William (d.1555), all of them mercers trading in Drapers' Row, now King Street. Two of Richard's sons and his son-in-law, William Pinner, each of whom was High Bailiff at least once, were among a small group of largely inter-related Aldermen and Councillors charged in the 1590s of misappropriating Corporation properties 'by kyndred, affinitie and major voyce'. This was part of a largely unsuccessful attempt to curb the powers of the elite, led by two disaffected members of the 12 and 25, John Crowther and Philip Bradford.

The 1461 charter had given the Corporation income from a number of sources, including the demesne lands, mills and tolls, and the annual payments of 12d from each burgage plot. Although voluminous lists of receipts and payments survive, the system of accounting makes it difficult to calculate total income and expenditure; but in 1528 income was about £55 and expenditure a little less, the major item being payment of annual fee farm to the Crown. In 1552 income was augmented by rents and fines from the Palmers' Guild estate, which in 1558 totalled £122 12s 1d, though by 1619 rents from all property – demesne and guild – had risen to over £200. In spite of the responsibilities that came with the transfer of Guild property – including the grammar school, Hosier's almshouses and support of the Preacher and Reader at the parish church – Ludlow was now a relatively wealthy borough. This can be seen by comparison with towns of similar size, for example Stratford-on-Avon, where the lands of the dissolved Guild of the Holy Cross brought the newly constituted Corporation an annual income of £80, with obligatory outgoings of £67. There is evidence, however, that the Corporation at Ludlow did not fully develop its endowment and enterprise may have been stifled by financial security.

The Corporation was served by salaried officials, the most important of whom was the Town Clerk. From 1546 to 1566 this office was held by John Alsopp, landlord of the Crown Inn, who also served as Low and High Bailiff, as Member of Parliament and, briefly, as Recorder; but none of his successors held elective office. Other officials included the two Sergeants-at-Mace, one for each bailiff, and the Common Sergeant, the senior of the three, who served both bailiffs. Lower in the hierarchy were a range of other employees, including the Town Crier and two beadles.

Corporation accounts illustrate its wide responsibilities. Street paving was often renewed, as in 1585, when 11s 4d was paid for 84 yards of paving in 'Galvord from the fryer gate upwards'. Public wells and conduits needed frequent maintenance, as did the springs and pipes which supplied them: in 1546 work on 'the pyppes in Corve Street' and in a 'close in galford' cost 3s. Other public services included the provision of standard weights and measures. Thomas Season in 1550 was paid 4d for 'three leaden weights for gylde hall'; and for the maintenance of the church clock, Thomas Rushbury received 10s in 1560 'for setting the clokes and chymes'.

Major building projects included a wooden bridge at Dinham, for which the 30s for 'making the new bridge' in 1540 is perhaps one of a series of payments. About 1570 the New House, a timber framed structure incorporating shops below and a handsome Council Chamber above, was built on the site of the present Buttercross. Many such buildings were erected in the early Elizabethan period, as enriched Corporations sought to express their civic identities, the Town Hall at Woodbridge (c.1575) and the Guildhall at Faversham (1574) being surviving examples. The New House had a first floor gallery facing Broad Street, where ls 6d was 'bestowed upon Mr secretary foxe in wyne and sugar'

St Julian's Well in Livesey Road, which gave its name to 'Wellhead' or 'Conduit' Field. From here Whitehall Brook ran to the Austin Friary. It was perhaps named after St Juliana of Nicomedia, who quenched the flames with which she was persecuted. The White Conduit in the Bull Ring, sketched by Henry Ziegler in the 1820s.

in 1572. Another expression of Ludlow's civic pride was its regalia, including two maces, first referred to in 1580, when 'Fennell the goldsmith' was paid for repairs. From 1600 new members had to present a silver spoon on election and by 1639 the civic plate included 'tunnes, saltes and bowles'.

The architectural style suggests a 15th or 16th century date but a public water tap was here much earlier, fed by piped water from St Julian's Well.

The Corporation spent heavily on what today would be called 'networking', as in 1559 when 'a potell of claret wyne' and 'a quart of malmesy and sugar' were gyven to 'the Justices of assices when they came throwe the towne from her(e)ford'. A less common occasion was in 1616, when 'wine bred & bere' were given to 'V of the kinges trumpitors ... passing into the northe to meet the king there'. There were many payments to entertainers, such as 6s 8d in 1540 'to the princes players for their play in the church', followed by 1s 6d 'for their play played at Alsoppes'. Just occasionally acts of human kindness are recorded, as in 1603, when Chamberlain Samuel Parker allowed 20s 'for the apellinge of Thomas Derby being father and motherless w(hi)ch I keepe'.

FIG.12

Part of the south side of Drapers' Row (now King Street), where most properties were owned by the Corporation, all but one of them transferred from the Palmers Guild in 1552. Except for No.18, which was rebuilt in the 19th century, these buildings retain their medieval frames, though these are visible externally only at No.19.

Nearly all the leaseholders, owners and tenants were drapers or mercers, cloths made in Ludlow being among their wares. Many of them were men of great influence in the Borough, Corporation members are marked + and those who were High Bailiff are marked *.

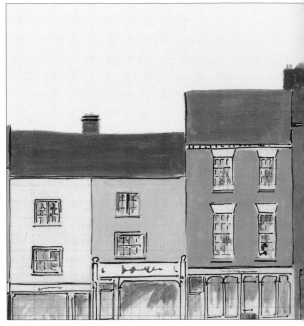

		14/15 King Street GUILD (FREEHOLD behind)	**16 King Street** GUILD
GUILD RENTAL 1525	leaseholder	Thom(a)s Crofton+	Thom(a)s lewis draper+
	property	too shopp(es) & An Entry	tene(men)t
	rent	xvs (15s)	xvs (15s)
	leaseholder		
	property		
	rent		
CORPORATION RENTAL 1619	leaseholder	Mr Th(omas) Crowther★	Mr Horne
	property	2 shops entry buttery	house & shop
	occupier(s)	Mr Aston★ Mr Stead★ Mr Turford★	Mr John Aston★
	rent	11s	£1
	owner/leaseholder	Thomas Crowther	
	property	one burgage (behind)	
	rent	12d	

17 King Street DEMSNE	18 King Street GUILD	19 King Street GUILD	
	Willia(m) longford★ a New ten(emen) xls (40s)	John Bradshaw too shops xiiijs (14s)	★Walter Rogers★ a corn(er) shop xiijs iiijd (13s 4d)
	John Bradshaw★ seller und(er)★ viijd (8d)	hew goldsmythe a tenement (now 1 Broad Street) xvjs	
Mr Thom(as) Watkis+ wid(ow) peerce shop his house and shops W(illia)m Reynolds shop	Mr Tho(mas) Watkis+ & Rooms over them 8d £2 00 00	Mr Samuel Lloyd★ Corn(er) shop £1 10s	
		Mr Horne one house & shop (now 1 Broad Street) 16s	

The Renter's Accounts after 1552 show how the Corporation discharged the responsibilities taken over from the Palmers Guild. In 1587, for example, out of an income from rents of about £260, nearly £118 went in regular payments: £64 6s to salaries at the parish church, £29 13s 4d to salaries at the Grammar School and £24 in weekly payments to 'the poore' at Hosier's Almshouses. In addition, there were maintenance costs from time to time, as in 1572, when Symon Thornton, school-master, was allowed £4 16s 3d. 'for mending the conduits and repairing the Schoolhouse', or in 1573, when £3 2s 3d was spent 'emptying and repairing' the Almshouse privy!

The Corporation took these responsibilities seriously. In 1590 they resolved that the Bailiffs 'with ten of the Brethren and the Parson or Preacher or some other learned man of Ludlow' should yearly visit the school 'and see the same be kept duly in repair and also examine how the Scholars profit in their learning by the good industry of the Schoolmaster and Usher'. The school flourished, as did many grammar schools at this time, giving a classical education not just to the sons of burgesses but also to those of the local gentry. As elsewhere, the educational system as a whole was limited, though there were some teachers who taught basic literacy, as Thomas Harrison, 'Master of the Children', perhaps did in the room over Broad Gate which he leased from the Corporation. Among the elite, however, cultural standards were high, with 22 testators naming books and/or musical instruments in this period, among them Richard Sparcheford, mercer, who had books and instruments in 1480.

By contemporary standards, the administration of Hosier's Almshouse was effi-cient, but after the dissolution of the religious houses, this was not enough to meet the needs of the poor, increasingly a social problem after 1550. Rating for poor relief began in 1563, and records show that in 1566 there were 38 recipients in two of the town's wards. The statutory system was supplemented by private charity, some of it through wills – between 1550 and 1600 a third of Ludlow testators gave money to the poor. In 1590 Charles Foxe endowed more almshouses in Corve Street, but with only four chambers, two of which were for people from Bromfield. After 1600, the proportion of wills benefiting the poor dropped to under a quarter, and though the Corporation sometimes showed compassion, this was more often to relatives of for-mer members than to the destitute.

Parliamentary representation

The majority of Ludlow's Members of Parliament were local men, many of whom also became High Bailiff. From the outset, however, a few had wider political significance, beginning in 1471 with Piers Beaupie, who was Cofferer to Edward IV. During the reign of Henry VIII, representation was dominated by the lawyer William Foxe of Ludford and his sons, who benefited greatly from the dissolution of the reli-

William Foxe (d.1554), member for Ludlow in the Parliaments of 1529 and 1536, depicted in armour of a rather old-fashioned design on a brass in the Foxe aisle of Ludford church.

gious houses. The Foxes became closely involved with the Council of the Marches, as was Robert Blount, Sergeant at Arms, elected in 1547. Under Mary other local gentry and Council officials were sometimes elected, perhaps because Ludlow burgesses were reluctant to be involved in national politics at that time.

During Elizabeth's long reign, all the M.P.s elected for Ludlow lived in the borough, a distinction shared only by Bath, Bristol, Newcastle-on-Tyne and Worcester. This was a notable achievement at a time when nearly all parliamentary boroughs - there were 175 by 1584 - had local gentry or complete outsiders holding at least one of their two seats. Ludlow, in fact, preserved this independence until 1614, though only after the 1597 election of the Lord President's secretary had been over-turned by the Commons. Most of the Ludlow burgesses elected were tradesmen, such as Robert Mason, tanner, and Thomas Candland, mercer, but William Poughnill of The College and Robert Berry of Castle Lodge were officials of the Council of the Marches, the latter sitting in six parliaments from 1584 to 1614.

After 1614, one seat was always occupied by a person associated with the Council in the Marches, the longest serving being Ralph Goodwin, Deputy Secretary and Clerk from 1626. Persons from outside the borough took the other seat, though one of these, Richard Tomlins who lived near London, had been born in Ludlow. In 1640, however, Tomlins' place was taken by Charles Baldwyn of Elsich near Ludlow, the start of a long tradition of representation of Ludlow by local landowning gentry.

Crime and Punishment

The 1461 charter gave Ludlow its own Town Court, with the authority to give capital sentences. The court met often – sometimes weekly – and was presided over by the Bailiffs, though from 1626 Capital Masters, usually former bailiffs, were appointed as additional magistrates. Malefactors were brought to court by the Sergeants and also by the constables, law-enforcing officers appointed annually for each ward. Each ward also held its court leet, where a local jury dealt with public nuisances such as stray pigs, piles of dung and scolding wives.

A calendar of prisoners for lst July, 1630, shows the range of cases which came before the Town Court. Francis Vaughan was sentenced to be hanged for 'picking purses', and William Price, tailor, and Alice Pearce, wife of a sawyer, were whipped for theft. John Lewis, tailor, was charged with rape, but found not guilty. Richard Langford, petty chapman, was bailed for £20 'to answer for living with' another man's wife and 'having children by her', while Richard Cooke was charged with saying 'he cared not a fart for Mr Bailiffs'. Drunken brawls were commonplace, as in 1629 when two glovers had 'opprobrious words' in The Angel 'about a flagon of ale while they played at cards', resulting in 'many blows'. Ludlow had the same barbaric punishments as other Tudor and Stuart towns. Prisoners awaiting trial were kept in squalor in the Tower at Galdeford Gate. Executions took place on what is still called Gallows' Bank, with the gibbet visible from many parts of the town.

There was a whipping post at the Market House but some prisoners were flogged though the town behind a cart, as was Elizabeth Fisher in 1604. A pillory was at the top of Mill Street, while stocks were movable around the town. There was also a gumble or ducking stool, used in 1600 for Mary Derby of Lower Broad Street, 'a drunkard, swearer, curser and common scold'.

Gallows' Bank in the eastern suburbs of Ludlow, a much valued public amenity in the midst of a residential area. The gibbet stood on the skyline, close to where there is now a break in the trees.

Buildings and life-style

The will and inventory of Walter Hubbold, made before August 1501, illustrate the house and living standard of a leading Ludlow citizen. Four rooms are listed - hall, parlour, chamber and kitchen. Meals were eaten in the hall, where there were trestles, cushions, and 'a forme'. The parlour had the best bed, valued at 7s 4d, but four expensive gowns, two of them made of 'London tawney' and 'London russet', were kept in the chamber - as were wool worth £3 and woad (for dyeing) worth £6 13s 4d. These three rooms had 'hangings', probably tapestries or painted cloth. There was a well equipped kitchen, which had brass as well as pewter items. Plate worth £15 14s 4d and the inventory total of £179 10s 4d indicate Hubbold's prosperity and that of the cloth industry with which he was clearly involved, though £140 of his wealth was credit from 'divers men'.

Though pre-1642 inventories are rare for Hereford diocese, wills show that the rooms cited above occurred in many houses. The arrangement was often like that at St John's House, built for the Foxes about 1540. A hall range originally open to the roof was bounded by a two storey cross wing, converted out of the former Hospital chapel, which had a parlour below and a chamber above; while the kitchen may have been detached, or at 'the lower end', where there is now an extension. As part of the post-medieval improvement in domestic comfort, halls were often divided into two storeys, as fireplaces replaced open hearths. The many chambers in some houses - William Gregory, shoemaker, had three in 1572 - suggests that horizontal division went on at Ludlow, as it certainly did by 1625, when Edmund Marsh, another shoemaker and Mary Pingle each had a 'chamber over the hall'. Some houses acquired the luxury of panelling. Richard Wadley, tanner, had 'waynscott' and 'paynted cloths' in 1587, but parlours were still used as bedrooms late in the period, Elinor Harding having a bedstead there in 1631.

St John's House, on the site of the former hospital chapel.
The gothic arch, now much restored, was perhaps the south entrance into the nave.

A view of the Reader's House c.1925, showing the timber framed porch which was built against the medieval stone elevation in 1616. The other side of the building is mid-sixteenth century timber framing, looking out over an enclosed garden.

A drawing of The Feathers in 1838 by William Twopenny of London, showing the doorway in the protruding entrance bay, in its original position. The sixteenth century building on the left, a smith's shop in 1839, was once The Griffin Inn.

Ludlow's association with the Council in the Marches caused more large houses to be built than would normally have been the case in a medium sized town. Some of these were in Castle Street, described by the Shrewsbury poet Thomas Churchyard in 1587 as a kind of piazza:

> On every side thereof fayre houses are,
> That makes a shew, to please both mynd and eye.

One of these houses, 'the fayre house of Maister Sackford', still stands as Castle Lodge, though the upper storey was added later by Robert Berry, like Thomas Sackford a Council official. An even larger house was that around what is now Quality Square, described by Churchyard as 'a fayre house that Maister Secretarie Foxe did bestowe greate charges on'. This house had a long gallery for display and entertainment, a rare feature in a town house. Other houses in Castle Street accommodated Council personnel, one of them on the site of Ludlow College, bought by Sir Richard Lewkener (d. 1616), Chief Justice of Chester. There were comparable houses elsewhere in the town. Other 'fayre' houses noted by Churchyard were the mansion built by Edmund

96

Castle Lodge, the lower parts of which were built in the early 1570s by Thomas Sackford, 'servant' to Sir Henry Sidney and Steward of Ludlow Castle, though incorporating an arched doorway from an earlier building on the site.

A view of the front of the two burgages plots, each 49 feet wide, on which Charles Foxe (d.1590) built a huge house of brick and stone round a central courtyard. In the eighteenth century the property was divided and mostly rebuilt in different styles.

Walter (d.1592), Chief Justice of South Wales, just inside Broad Gate; and the house at the Austin Friary, occupied in 1587 by Henry Townsend (d.1621), Justice of Chester. A smaller house was in the Bull Ring, that of Thomas Hackluit (d.1544), Clerk to the Council, now The Feathers Hotel. This was lavishly refronted and decorated in 1619 by Rees Jones (d.1656), a Welsh attorney who enjoyed a profitable career in the Council's courts. His brother-in-law, Edward Waties (d.1635), a member of the Council, lived opposite in a house that had a gallery and at least six chambers. Another spacious house was that in the churchyard, now called The Reader's House. The medieval stone walls were part of the house of Thomas Cookes (d.1513), Esq., who had been Servitor to Prince Arthur. There was considerable rebuilding in the 1550 s, and in 1616 an imposing three storey porch was added to the churchyard frontage by Thomas Kaye, Chaplain to the Council.

These houses had sophisticated interiors, some features of which survive, such as the ornate plaster ceiling in the former Great Chamber at The Feathers; the original panelling in a room at Castle Lodge; and the Renaissance mural at Barnaby House in Mill Street, the town residence of the descendants of Thomas Barnaby (d.1471), Treasurer to Edward IV.

At lower social levels, several buildings remain from this period, though often altered or disguised. One of them is the well preserved undercroft and open hall at Nos. 14 and 15 King Street, with encroaching shops and chambers in front. These were all rebuilt in the later 15th century, though earlier buildings were there before 1330. There are late medieval timber-framed houses in Corve Street, including No. 62, which preserves blocked entrances from hall to service rooms, and No.112, once part of 'the Great House' of Thomas Clungunwas (d.1555), clothier. No.56 Old Street, later Lane's Asylum, was once the home of Thomas Wheeler, M.P. for Ludlow in 1539 and 1552, perhaps the reason why the plaster-work arms of King Edward VI embellish the hall. At No.5 Old Street, behind a later brick front, are the richly moulded ceiling beams of the former Red Lion Inn. The most impressive legacy of the period, however, is the scale of building in the congested town centre, where three and four storey buildings, accommodating cellars, shops and chambers, still soar upwards in the Bull Ring, on the north side of High Street and in upper Broad Street. In contrast – as in most towns – the houses of poor people rarely survive, though tiny Springfield Cottage, in St John's Lane, may be from the early 17th century.

Most of these buildings were timber-framed, a brick house at No.46 Bull Ring still being unusual enough to be called 'the brick house' in a pre-Civil war lease. Of the 18 builders identified for 1614-24, seven were carpenters, the most prosperous of whom was Thomas Boseley (d.1645). They were part of a distinctive Ludlow school of carpentry, which in the early 17th century produced scroll decoration, richly carved brackets, lozenges of diamond struts and quatrefoil panels that combine to give an appearance of opulence – and sometimes of ostentation – to buildings of this period.

Nos.14-15 Raven Lane, which in 1619 belonged to Mr Edward Colbatch (d.1640), shoemaker, a member of the Corporation. The house exemplifies the Ludlow style after c.1600, decoration intensifying with height. The bracket is a restrained Sheila-na-gig, a fertility symbol!

CHAPTER SIX

1642-1660: CIVIL WAR AND INTERREGNUM

The build up of hostilities

In Ludlow as elsewhere, grievances had been developing for some years, especially over taxation, and in 1640 the town was short by £30 of its payment of a tax to finance the Scottish war. In 1641 there was the additional discontent about Parliament's abolition of the Council in the Marches. The Corporation protested that since the Council's jurisdiction had been questioned, 'there has been little resort to the said town', but criminal business ceased that year and civil matters in 1642.

As throughout the rural west, most Ludlow people were instinctively Royalist. Those who were fined after the war for fighting against Parliament included a number of tradesmen, at least seven of whom were in the leather trades, including William Colbach, corviser, and the two sons of Edward Powis, tanner and alderman. Even some of the town's Puritans, such as Cuthbert Hely, once of the Signet Office, supported the King, though others, like the lawyer John Aston, were zealously for Parliament. Most local gentry, like the Herberts and the Foxes, were Royalist, as were nearly all the employees of the Council of the Marches, including Ralph Goodwyn, Ludlow's M.P. A few, however, were for Parliament, including Sir Robert Harley of Brampton Bryan, who was active on committees of the Long Parliament before the war began, and was later known as 'the iconoclast' for his part in destroying stained glass windows in London. Most Ludlow families known to have fought in the war were on the same side, but internal divisions did occur, as with the sons of John Price, a chapman from Holdgate Fee, one of whom, Avery, was a Parliamentary soldier, while another, Robert, was 'of the King's party'.

The course of the war in and around Ludlow, 1642-46

Ludlow was a Royalist stronghold throughout. There were a few local incidents and skirmishes, but the first serious threat came in May 1643, probably from an army led by Sir William Waller which briefly occupied Hereford. Inhabitants in the suburbs were ordered to build ramparts, while the town walls were repaired, 'loopholes for muskets' were made through the gates, and 'fires and coles' were voted for watchmen.

Ludlow Castle was of considerable strategic importance. The defence was undertaken by 'foreign soldiers', including a detachment of Irish troops under Captain John Davalier, a Florentine mercenary. An undated paper lists 28 'voyd houses' available to billet soldiers, including Castle Lodge and the house of Rees Jones, now The Feathers. As compensation for the litigants who had once flocked to the Council of the Marches, the war years brought new visitors to Ludlow. Some were refugees from areas controlled by Parliament, such as Dr Warner, Bishop of Rochester. The most distinguished was the King, who came from Cardiff with 300 horsemen on 7 August 1645. Three shillings were given to the bell ringers, twice the amount given in 1644 'for ringinge Prince Rupert in to Towne'. Public opinion was hostile to those who flaunted Parliamentary opinions, so that Thomas Vaughan of Tewkesbury, who was 'well affected to Parliament', was unable to collect his rent from the King's Arms in the Bull Ring 'without great danger or hazard of life'.

Locally as well as nationally, the course of the war went against the Royalists, though they did capture Parliamentary outposts at Brampton Bryan and Hopton Castle, the latter with much savagery. Shrewsbury was taken by the Parliamentarians in 1645, and Bridgnorth on 26 April 1646. Earlier that month Colonel John Birch, a Bristol merchant turned Parliamentarian commander, was ordered to Ludlow. His troops combined with others from Radnorshire and Shropshire to provide over 1000 foot and 600 horse. The defenders, commanded by Sir Michael Woodhouse, were only 250 foot and 100 horse.

The siege began on 24 April, when the Parliamentarians forced the enemy into the town. Birch had a siege camp south east of Ludlow, perhaps at Caynham. In anticipation of bombarding the castle his men may have dug the trenches which survive on Whitcliffe, though it is doubtful if the guns ever arrived. Detachments sent to relieve the garrison on 29 April were beaten back, but the number of soldiers buried in the area – nine at Bromfield in May – suggests that fighting continued sporadically. By mid-May negotiations were taking place, and on 20 May a letter was received in London reporting 'an absolute agreement' for surrender on 1 June, 'the officers to march away with horses and arms and the common soldiers without arms'. It is likely, however, that the date was moved to 26 May, for it is recorded that the siege lasted 33 days.

This agreement spared Ludlow the devastation suffered at places such as Bridgnorth. The war disrupted the town's economy, however, and the population dropped sharply from the 2,600 estimated for 1641, though arguably much of this was due to the cessation of the Council in the Marches. The war's saddest legacy was the destruction of many properties, in the suburbs and in the town. This may have begun in 1643, when houses were demolished so that Royalists could have a clear field of fire from the walls while the attackers were denied shelter for setting explosives. Places where this happened included Corve Street, where the Bailiffs were ordered in October 1645 to 'survey the demolished houses', and in Castle Street and Dinham, where title deeds of a house opposite the castle describe it as 'pulled down' in the wars. A second phase of destruction was indiscriminate burning in the suburbs, much of which occurred on 24 April 1644, when, for example, the house at 43 Lower Galdeford 'was burnt to the ground by wicked command of Sir Michael Woodhouse'.

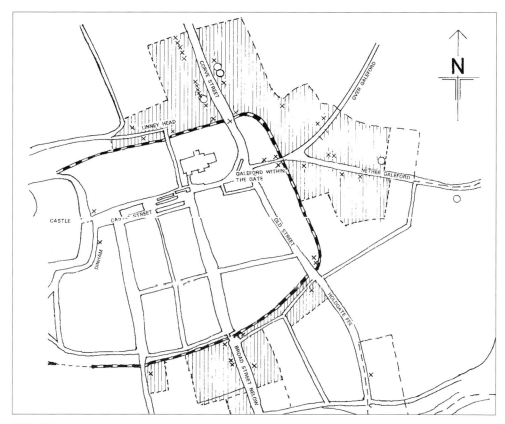

FIG: 13 Civil War damage in Ludlow

○   Buildings later demolished

✕   Hessplaces and demolished buildings (perhaps by not necessarily destroyed by fire)

      Areas where tenural reconstructions shows extensive Civil War damage, with many 'void' sites after 1646

━━━━ The town walls

– – – The parish boundary

The Interregnum 1646–1660

Ludlow had to adapt to the new regimes which followed the King's defeat in 1646, culminating in the Commonwealth from 1649. Most members of the Corporation kept their places, but outside influences had more power over the town than previously, including the new County Committees, and these ensured that committed Parliamentarians held key positions. Foremost among them were John Aston, lawyer, and Captain William Botterell, one of a series of governors of Ludlow Castle. Both were High Bailiff twice and both served in Parliament, Aston for Ludlow in 1654 and 1656 and Botterell as one of two County members in the 'Barebones' Parliament of 1653. Another appointment was that of Major William Braine, an extreme Republican who had been a witness at the King's trial, who was Town Clerk from 1646 to 1657. Little is known of the views of the Rectors at this time, but at least two Preachers were Puritans, one of them Richard Sadler, who had returned from New England. Several of the 11 Masters at the Grammar School from 1648 to 1659 were known Puritans.

There were constant reminders of the new order. New maces were made bearing the Commonwealth insignia, while at the parish church the King's Armes were 'washt out'. The organ pipes were melted down and its case dismantled, but the bells were used for Government propaganda, as on 2 January 1654 when the Wardens paid 2s 6d. 'for ringing for joy when Lord Cromwell was made Protector'. Many of the town's best houses were occupied by Parliamentarians, including Sir Robert Harley in the large house of the Foxes round what is now Quality Square.

Such evidence as is available suggests that the pace of economic and demographic recovery was gentle. Priority was given to replacing burnt houses, and 19 of the 39 leases issued for Corporation properties in the war-damaged areas between 1646 and 1660 had incentives for quick rebuilding. Thus in 1649 John Cleobury was granted the property which is now The Compasses with 'no fine but to build'. Yet rebuilding was often slow, partly, no doubt, because the reduced population lowered the demand for houses. The property outside Broad Gate which is now The Wheatsheaf was leased to Thomas Price in 1655 with the usual 'condition to build', but nine years later the lease was re-issued to William Woodall, carpenter, in similar terms, and work was not finished until 1668.

CHAPTER SEVEN

1660-1832: URBAN RENAISSANCE

For many towns these were years of growth and buoyancy. Agriculture and manufacturing flourished, and much of the resulting trade flowed through the towns, the established centres of exchange. The shops and professional services of towns were sought by the enriched members of society, especially the land-owning gentry, many of whom now owned or rented town houses. Classical styles of architecture became fashionable and there was a mania for urban improvement. The term 'Urban Renaissance' has been coined to describe these and related processes.

In general terms Ludlow conformed to this pattern, with population rising from an estimated 2,000 in 1676 to 5,253 in 1831, most of the increase coming after 1760. However, the revival of the Council of the Marches gave Ludlow a distinctive character during the first part of this period - and helped to shape its later development.

The Council of the Marches, 1661-1689

Following representations from Ludlow Corporation in July 1660, just two months after Charles II landed at Dover, and petitions 'numerously signed' from many parts of Wales, the Council of the Marches was re-established on 9 September, 1661. It was, however, for civil matters only, and with jurisdiction over Wales alone, not the border counties. The first Lord President, Richard Vaughan, second Earl of Carbery of Golden Grove, Carmarthenshire, began by acting firmly to 'appease tumults' but later there were complaints of misappropriation of funds. In 1684 his successor, Henry Somerset, Duke of Beaufort, sought to boost the Council's prestige by a spectacular 'Progress' through Wales; but when, in 1687, he summoned Welsh magistrates to Ludlow, more than half stayed away.

By 1689 the Council's unpopularity was widespread and there were nearly 18,000 signatures to a petition that the Council was 'a great expense to the Crown and no advantage to it'. A prayer of the time ended with the words: From the plague, pestilence and Ludlow Court, Good lord deliver us. It suited the new government of William and Mary to centralise administration in London and on 25 July 1689 the Council was formally dissolved.

The number of identified people associated with the Council totals 85, including 14 judges, five other members and 33 officials. Many lived far from Ludlow, some of them employing deputies, but 34 were in or near the town. Among them were Sergeant Timothy Littleton and Sir Job Charlton, both of whom were M.P.s for Ludlow. Littleton, one of a distinguished family of Shropshire jurists, left in 1670 to be a Baron of the Exchequer, but Charlton, described as 'an old cavalier, loyal, learned, grave and wise', remained a formidable local force until after 1689. The proportion of Ludlow residents was highest among office holders – Chetwyds, Huntons, Purefoys, Wigmores and Winwoods – who formed a close-knit social group which stayed in Ludlow after 1689. Most Councillors lived out of town, but Humphrey Cornewall of Berrington, appointed in 1670, occupied Brand House.

Many of the most illustrious Ludlow families after 1660, living in some of the largest houses, were there because of pre-Civil war links with the Council. Robert Berry, Esq., of Castle Lodge, with 12 hearths in 1672, had married Dame Katherine Howard, widow of the fifth son of the Earl of Suffolk. The Lloyds, who came from Maesyfelin in Cardiganshire, had a 13 hearth house in Broad Street, and brought some of their relatives to Ludlow, including Lady Cornwallis of Abermarlais, Carmarthenshire, who died in 1719 and was 'splendidly interred' in St. Laurence's.

Sketches of Ludlow Castle by Thomas Dineley, who accompanied the Duke of Beaufort on his progress in 1684:
1: The main domestic buildings, seen from the north. To the right is the hall, with its three large windows. Banquets and ceremonial occasions were held here. To the left of the hall is the gardrobe tower, with suites of residential rooms. The main court room was in the Great Chamber block, behind this tower. There were further lodgings to the left.
2: The inner bailey from the west, showing a drawbridge and the gabled roofs of The Governor's House.

Ludlow Society

More is known about the composition of Ludlow society during the eighteenth century than at any previous period. This is due to the survival of an informative series of Easter Books, in which the annual church tithe or lewn was recorded by the parish clerk. The assessments, usually made by Church Wardens, took note of the perceived circumstances of each household and can therefore be used as an index of social and economic standing. Adult sons and daughters, relatives, residential servants and apprentices are all recorded, though younger children - probably those under sixteen - are omitted. A feature is the inclusion of lodgers or sojourners, many of whom were part of Ludlow households at this time.

Householders are listed by initial letter for each ward, with assessments ranging, in 1724 for example, from £11s to 3d. In most cases occupation is given or social standing indicated by such prefixes as Esq., Mr or Mrs. Correlation with other records suggests that nearly all Ludlow residents are included, from the richest to those at the almshouses, though a few of the very poor or destitute are omitted. Late in the century, entries in the Easter Books became more casual, but from 1717, the first surviving entry, until about 1770, Ludlow households can be reconstructed in a way not normally available to urban historians for this period.

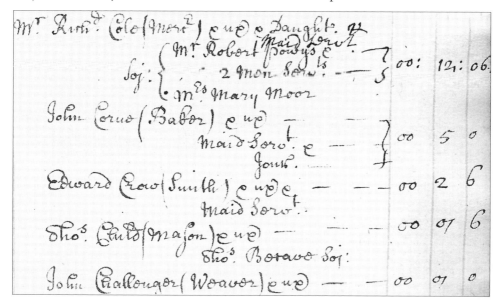

Part of the 1724 Easter Book for Old Street ward. This extract covers a wide social range, from Richard Cole, a prosperous mercer, and his wife (ux), daughter and gentry sojourners, down to John Challenger and his wife, a weaver of modest means and social position.

FIG. 14

**Status and occupational groups in Ludlow in 1763, based on the Easter Book
(in which the annual payments of church rates were recorded)**

| Group | No. | Church Lewn (tax) | | Servants | Window tax | | Corporation |
		No.	Mean	Mean	No.	Mean	
Greater gentry	22	21	14s 8d	1.7	19	16	5
Professions	27	23	7s 2d	1.1	17	21	8
Lesser gentry	62	51	6s 10d	.5	30	14	3
Mercers/booksellers	9	9	6s 2d	1.4	9	16	2
Total	**120**						
Innkeepers with servants	20	18	3s 11d	1.8	19	16	-
Leather trades	19	17	3s 10d	.6	15	9	-
Other dealers	31	31	3s 0d	.6	26	9	-
Food trades	31	29	2s 6d	.7	26	8	-
Master glovers	16	16	2s 4d	.6	14	9	-
Building operatives	21	18	2s 2d	.2	16	9	-
Metal/wood trades	31	28	1s 10d	.2	31	9	1
Services (including transport)	25	18	1s 8d	.1	16	8	-
Innkeepers with no servants	26	25	1s 8d	-	26	8	-
Making clothes/shoes	32	30	1s 7d	.1	19	8	-
Manufacture of cloth	13	11	1s 6d	.2	6	7	-
Total	**265**						
Journeyman glovers/gloveresses	31	13	10d	-	5	7	-
Other journeymen	58	43	9d	-	12	7	-
Labourers	69	38	8d	-	7	7	-
No trade or title	97	61	8d	-	2	7	-
Alms-persons	48	29	4d	-	-	-	-
Total	**303**						
GRAND TOTAL	**688**						

In Figure 14 above, heads of households in 1763 have been categorised into groups, adapting classifications used for other towns to meet the situation at Ludlow. These groups have been listed in rank order by the mean of the lewn paid, and other criteria have been shown for comparative purposes: the number of servants per household, the mean number of windows on the window tax assessment of 1763, and the number of persons serving on the Corporation.

Figure 14 suggests that there were three broad strata of Ludlow society, though with substantial internal differences. At the top was a group of families who lived in the largest houses and dominated the Corporation places then held by Ludlow residents. This group can be called the establishment. Some way below in terms of perceived wealth and house size - except for the innkeepers, some of whom kept very large premises - were a wide variety of dealers, manufacturers and craftsmen, constituting nearly two-fifths of recorded households. All of these seem to have been self-employed. Below them was a slightly larger group forming the base of the social pyramid, some of whom were journeymen, while others were those whom one historian has described as 'the still scarcely explored ranks of day labourers and the urban poor'. All these seem to have worked for others, were unemployed or dependent on charity.

There was certainly some movement between the groups. An extreme example is that of Volant Vashon Ballard (1776-1832), son of a journeyman glover, who became a Vice-Admiral in the Royal Navy, and whose son married a daughter of Richard Salwey, Esq., of Moor Park. The Salweys were one of several land-owning families who had houses in Ludlow and were at the very heart of its establishment. There was also transition the other way, for example John Beebe Morris, an attorney in the 1820s, who was later in Hosier's Almshouses. Within each stratum of society, however, there were strong kinship networks, and dynasties occurred at all social levels.

The balance between the groups was also flexible. In spite of the dissolution of the Council of the Marches in 1689, the number of establishment families increased from about 65 in 1667 to over 120 in 1724. Occasionally manufacturers joined this elite, such as Mr Samuel Waring, a wholesale glover, reputedly worth £20,000 when he died. In 1724 his lewn assessment was 10s, he had a 27 window house and employed 4 servants. He was on the Corporation from 1707 to 1744, serving twice as High Bailiff. At the other end of the social scale, the proportion of those who worked for others seems to have risen later in the period. The number of the poor also rose, and were increasingly vulnerable to food shortages or economic crises. In January 1789 a subscription was opened for bread to be distributed weekly 'among the necessitous poor', while in 1816 a public meeting was convened to consider 'the present distressed state of the poor'.

The Establishment

The largest group were the gentry from the surrounding countryside. Some of these, like the Barnabys of Bockleton, were of great antiquity. Some had achieved their status through the law, including the Powys's of Henley Hall, descendants of a Ludlow tanner. Others rose through commerce, among them the Powells of Stanage Park, descended from a Tudor merchant adventurer. A few families became rich through the rural iron industry, especially the Knights, who acquired the furnace and forge at Bringewood, four miles from Ludlow on the River Teme, in 1698. Other gentry came from further afield, such as the Gwynns of Garth in Breconshire, who tenanted a number of Ludlow houses from the 1740s.

Many heads of Ludlow gentry households were widows, such as Mrs Ann Kettleby of Neen Savage, widow of a former Recorder and M.P. for Ludlow, who lived in a large house in Castle Street in 1724. Others were spinsters, such as Isabella Sprott and sister in Broad Street in 1770, two of several Ludlow members of a family that came from the Marsh, near Much Wenlock. Widows, spinsters, and bach-

The rear of Brand House in Ludlow, which was used as a town house by the Walcots in the first half of the 18th century. In 1724 the residents were Mr and Mrs George Walcot, with 'a kinswoman' and four servants. George was the second son of George Walcot of Walcot.

Walcot Hall, before it was rebuilt after purchase by Lord Clive in 1764. The Walcots had held land in Lydbury North since the 12th century. The house, perhaps built by Humphrey Walcot (1545-1616), a rich London merchant, had a gabled front, with a lower range and later, stables behind.

A detail of Samuel Scott's 1766 painting of Broad Street, showing two members of the gentry. On the right is Alexander Stuart (d.1782), Governor of Ludlow Castle. He claimed kinship with the royal Stuarts and spent much of his time in Scotland. On the left is Miss Harriett Price (d.1807). When she died she left a 'King Charles Picture set in Diamonds', suggesting she too had Stuart sympathies.

elors were often lodgers in large Ludlow households, such as Madam Alice Herbert, daughter of Henry Herbert, Baron of Chirbury, one of five gentlewomen lodging in Drapers' Row (now King Street) with Thomas Haughton, mercer, in 1692.

Many Ludlow professional men were related to the gentry. After 1689 there were usually six or seven attorneys in the town. In 1724 these included John Baldwin of Munslow, and John Holland, son of John Holland of Brimfield Court. The law remained a route for social advance, an example being Somerset Davies (1715-81), attorney, who was described by Lybbe Powis in 1771 as 'a gentleman of large fortune'. Somerset was the son of a Ludlow mercer, and his own son bought Croft Castle, becoming M.P. and Sheriff of Herefordshire. Another prominent lawyer was Benjamin Karver (1665-1737), from Upton, Little Hereford, who lived at Castle Lodge.

There was a similar number of medical men, with at least one physician, and some surgeons and apothecaries. In 1798 there were three physicians, one of them Dr Babbington – later a noted botanist – and another Dr Martin Dunne, a relative of the Dunnes of Gatley Park. Surviving papers of Dr Dunne, at Ludlow from 1770 to 1814, show him to have used electric treatment and other advanced techniques. In the 1820s a young surgeon, Henry Hickman of Bromfield, was in the town for a few years, probably at 114 Corve Street, and was a pioneer of anaesthesia.

Other members of the establishment included leading mercers, such as Tamberlaine Davies (d.1685), whose shop goods were worth £527. There were retired or half -pay navy and army officers and, after 1700, excise officers and others in 'the new professions'. Some rural clergy lived part of the year in Ludlow, such as Revd. Sneade of Bedstone (d.1820), 'for the advantages of education and society' for his three daughters.

'Very good company'

When John Macky (d.1726), traveller, letter-writer and government agent, visited Ludlow in 1714, he referred to the 'very good company', highlighting 'the abundance of pretty ladies, well dressed, who came from the adjacent Counties, for the Conveniency and Cheapness of boarding'. Later, at Preston, he described that town as 'reckoned next to St Edmund's Bury, Ludlow and Beverley ... the prettiest retirement in England'. In 1744 another visitor remarked that 'here the gentry dress fine, live easily, visit much and do things very grand'. Ludlow, indeed, was sometimes compared to a county town, though in 1766 it was given a mixed encomium by Thomas Falconer of Chester, when he wrote: 'The town is most agreeably situated and if the principal street had less verdure in it, no County town would exceed it. But it is as dull as even Warwick'.

In 1784, however, Lord Byng, often a caustic commentator, called it 'one of the best towns for a genteel family of small fortune to retire to', while in 1805 William Mavor, a schoolmaster from Woodstock, wrote in his Tour through Wales that 'Ludlow's situation is universally and deservedly admired'.

These favourable impressions, qualified though they are, can be re-inforced by analysis of some of the taxes paid by Ludlow's wealthiest residents in the mid-eighteenth century. The results are set out in Fig.15, which ranks the Welsh border towns according to various criteria. Data of this kind seems to emphasise genteel and middle-class residence. Ludlow's high ranking - it was fourth for carriage and silver plate duties in 1756-62 and fifth for male servants' tax in 1780 - clearly shows its social status, all the other places in the first six being county towns. Using different criteria the historian Peter Borsay cites Ludlow as one of the places to be ranked, with county towns and some others, among those 'that were able to exert a major impact on an extensive hinterland'. Such towns come above smaller market towns like Farnham or Stratford-on-Avon, but below 'the handful of provincial capitals which constituted the elite cadre of the system' such as Bristol or Norwich. Of these second tier towns he has written:

'Lancashire had Preston, Derbyshire had Chesterfield, Lincolnshire had Stamford, Shropshire had Ludlow, Buckinghamshire had Aylesbury and Kent had Maidstone'.

110

FIG 15 Persons paying taxes on the Welsh border, mid 18th century

	Carriage duties 1756-62	Silver plate duty 1756-62	Male servants duty 1780
Shrewsbury	61	139	72
Worcester	48	138	66
Hereford	23	61	32
LUDLOW	11	40	27
Monmouth	9	14	32
Brecon	8	24	15
Bridgnorth	6	26	13
Droitwich	8	13	11
Leominster	5	13	7

Amenities and amusements for gentility

A subscription list for a new organ at St Laurence's in 1672 is the first evidence after the Restoration of interest in Ludlow as a cultural centre. Of the cost of £133 7s 2d, two-fifths came from the rural gentry, headed by Lord Herbert of Chirbury. Another early facility was the terrace walk at the north side of the church yard, where a seat is shown on a drawing of 1684 'The fine Prospect' from here was praised by Macky in 1714. Families and friends also walked in private gardens, 'being pleasant for Air', as when Ann Kettleby, it was claimed, was abducted by papists in 1697.

The castle had the best facilities for leisure in Ludlow, and these remained in use after 1689. A large bowling green is clearly marked on a plan drawn by William Stukeley the antiquarian in 1721 but there are earlier references. In 1700 a tailor was in a fight 'having been at the Castle waiting upon gentleman ... players who had been sent for to show some sport to several persons of quality'. In 1719 there was 'a splendid Ball' at the castle, given by a daughter of Sir Herbert Croft of Croft and attended by 'most of the Officers and other Gentlemen and Ladies of the best Quality in this town'. Other kinds of social life centred on the inns, and in 1713 itinerant players from Hereford performed at The Angel.

Soon after 1700 the Corporation rebuilt the Market Hall, with a long upper room. There is no evidence that this was then used for dancing assemblies, though three 'Waytes or Town Musicke' [presumably musicians] were appointed in 1706. As the castle deteriorated after 1720, however, there was a need to fit up the upper room. Walnut panelling was provided in 1724 and in 1725 Henry Arthur Herbert of

Oakly Park, seeking electoral votes in Ludlow, gave a new ceiling and floor boards and had the windows reglazed. Assemblies were now held regularly, the grandest being the Bailiffs' Balls on two nights in late October. There are many descriptions of Ludlow balls, as in 1771, when Mrs Lybbe Powis found the assembly 'tolerable with two lords and six baronets', and with 'many pretty women', though regretting that 'Lord Clive's family were at Spaw' and Lady Powis 'ill in London'.

Henry Herbert also promoted horse races on the Old Field at Bromfield, the first record of which is in 1725. There was a three day meeting in 1726, followed by 'Balls three Nights successive and handsome Entertainments for the gentlemen and Ladies, wholly at the expense of Henry Arthur Herbert, Esq.' The races remained an annual event, often with concerts, cock-fights and fives matches in the mornings, followed by ordinaries (meals for men) at mid-day and a ball each evening. Hunting was another robust sport. From the 1730s local estates were advertised as having good hunting, while there was a pack of Ludlow hounds by 1822. In 1788 ten Ludlow residents held game certificates, allowing them to shoot, while the River Teme was noted for its fish, encouraging Richard Bowlker, a Raven Lane shoemaker, to produce his best selling The Art of Angling in 1749.

Walks were other 'public arenas of display'. Before 1747 the Castle Ditch at

The Market Hall built in 1702, which had 'a long room' used for Assemblies and two other rooms on the upper floor. On Thursday, 27 December, 1811, those at a Winter Dancing Assembly included Lucien Bonaparte, brother of Napoleon, in Ludlow as a prisoner on parole. The Times reported that he did not dance, though some of his party did. He attended the Countess Powis to the supper rooms, after which he returned to the card room.

This detail from William Marlow's picture of Ludlow Castle, Mill and Weir shows people on walks which were laid out by the Earl and Countess of Powis in the early 1770s. The work was planned by John Elles, a Ludlow gardener, whose costs included £22 11s for 'trees for Ludlow new walk' in 1775.

Dinham was landscaped to provide 'the New Walk'. It had rails and gates and was also called 'the Mall'. In 1771 a promenade was laid out round the castle, giving 'picturesque views', while walks over Whitcliffe were also fashionable. Later, excursions elsewhere were popular, as to the Tea Gardens in what is now Julian Road. There was a theatre in Ludlow by the 1770s, with touring companies performing intermittently and celebrities sometimes on stage, such as Mr and Mrs Siddons in Othello in 1803. The town had a succession of booksellers, starting with Edward Robinson from the 1660s, and there was a circulating library by 1782.

For the privileged, life in Georgian and Regency Ludlow was very agreeable. In a memoir of her mother, 'the Belle of Ludlow' in the 1790's, Ellen Oliver wrote: Mary Sneade loved to tell ... of the pure fun and frivolity of her first Ludlow season... Broad Street gay with rapid feet and glancing eyes; the shopping expeditions for to-morrow's ball; the little encounters with partners from last night's ball ... It had all been so happy ... Charltons of Ludford, Rogers of Castle House, ... Lady Clive, the Oakleys of Oakley, the Brights of Tetterton, the Corbets of Longnor, the Knights of Downton ... Mother loved murmuring over the names dreamily.

Dealers, manufacturers and craftsmen

In the eighteenth century as now, most dealers had their premises on or close to the ancient spine of the town. The distribution of shops was more mixed than previously. In 1724 there were four mercers in Drapers' Row, but also two ironmongers, two booksellers and two apothecaries. The wealth of dealers varied widely. Of the twelve butchers in Ludlow in 1724, only three can be linked with inventories, all under £20, but by mid-century there were at least two wealthy butchers: William Crow (d. 1770), with goods worth nearly £1,500, and Thomas Morley (d.1773), described as 'an opulent butcher and grazier'.

Shops sold a wide range range of goods, from basic materials such as the 'tarroyle and pytch' stocked by Roger Latward, iron-monger in 1700, to delicacies such as the 'Bath, Chelsea and Dublin Bunns' served hot each morning by Catherine Sheriff, 'baker, pastry cook and confectioner', at her Tower Street shop in 1822. Saddlers stocked the leatherware needed by horses, such as the 'three pad sadles' worth £1 13s and the '12 horse collars' worth 13s 8d listed for James Pugh in 1724. In 1692 the stock of Richard Plummer, chandler, at his Bull Ring shop included chamber-pots, wine bottles, candles and 'Clee Hill ware'. The mercers offered a wide range of fabrics and furnishings, such as the German serges, Bath coatings and Turkey carpets on sale at Adams' Wholesale and Retail Drapery Warehouse in 1775.

In an age of 'rampant consumerism', links with the world of fashion were paraded, as by Elizabeth Cross, milliner, who described herself in 1775 as 'from Mrs Norman's, Tavistock Street, London'. She had just laid in 'a fresh and genteel Assortment of every article in the Millinery, Linen Drapery and Haberdashery branches', and also stocked 'Fine Teas, Coffee and Chocolate'.

Ludlow, like similar market towns, had a wide industrial base, with smiths, coopers, weavers, hatters, mantua-makers, shoemakers and tailors making goods for local consumption.

There were two or three clockmakers in Ludlow. One was Benjamin Tipton (d.1796), who was apprenticed to Thomas Nash of Shrewsbury in 1726. This Longcase Clock, inscribed B. Tipton, Ludlow, was sold for £4,100 in 1993.

114

There were up to ten bakers, using flour ground at the town mills. Two of the mills once used for fulling cloth now had other uses. For much of the period white paper was made at Steventon Mill, described in 1719 as having 26 hammers; while for much of the 18th century, silk was manufactured at one of the Mill Street mills. A trade of growing importance was malting, recently described as 'the most character-istic of market town manufactures'. By 1770 there were 18 malting businesses in the town, and by 1828 the number had risen to 30. There were many malthouses, especially in Corve Street.

This view of Ludlow from the new railway station in the 1850s shows commercial properties behind Corve Street, among them the malthouse of the Hand family with its distinctive kiln.

The Malthouse and kiln survive, behind what is now 139a Corve Street though now used for other purposes. The tiled floor on which the malt was dried in the kiln is still there.

Glove manufacturing

Glove manufacture thrived in the central Welsh Marches, with Leominster and Ludlow the major centres. Exact figures are not available, but at times the area seems to have been comparable in importance to the Yeovil and Woodstock regions, though Worcester was the foremost glove-making centre. In 1832, when Princess Victoria and her mother visited Ludlow, they each received two pairs of gloves: 'the principal manufacture of the town'. Fig. 16, recording the admission of glovers to the Stitchmens' Guild, illustrates how manufacturing grew in importance, with expan-sion from 1660 and a peak after 1700. Structural changes in the industry, however, mean that the apparent later decline has to be interpreted with caution, though production did drop sharply in the 1830s.

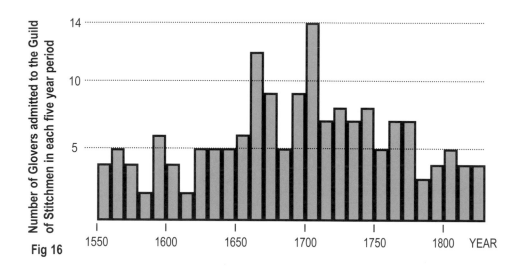

Fig 16

There were a number of master glovers, who employed journeymen - often to cut out the gloves from processed leather - and gloveresses and children to sew the gloves. In 1697 the industry was said to be 'a great support to poor people...in or near Ludlow'. In 1724 there were 15 masters, 25 journyemen and 24 gloveresses, but the number of outworkers is unknown. One glover of this time, Samuel Waring (d.1744), described as a wholesaler, owned many estates and was said to be worth £20,000. In 1811 it was claimed in Felton's *A Description of the Town of Ludlow* that 'the number of men, women and children employed amounts to several hundred'. This was supported in 1815 by a survey showing that 735 persons were employed by twelve masters, of whom 90% were women and children. During the Napoleonic Wars the trade boomed, with an estimated 365,000 pairs of gloves produced yearly, many for markets in London and the United States.

A variety of skins were used, such as the 200 sheep pelts bought by James Harris in 1694. Humphrey Blithe, in 1708, had other materials, including oil, wool and glue. The links with other leather trades were close, especially with leather dyers such as Mary Pea, whose stock in 1817 included the dyes ochre and umber. A wide range of gloves was produced, as shown by the inventory of William Willmott in 1662, which included 32 pairs of 'mens kidd', 81 pair of 'womens kidd' and 20 pair of 'childrens' kidd', worth respectively £1 15s, £4 1s. and 12s 6d.

The industry was regulated by the Stitchmen's Guild, governed by the elected Six Men. They protected members against other traders selling gloves, as attempted by the mercers and milliners in 1691. In 1697 they joined with glovers from Leominster, Kington, Weobley and elsewhere to petition the Government against a duty on oil, alum and leather. In 1724 they banned George Somers 'from following

116

the trade of a glover and skinner', he 'not having served an apprenticeship' - though he was later admitted after paying a £5 fine. Their main task, however, was the admission of new members, and here the most remarkable feature is their insularity. Of 118 glovers admitted as freemen after 1660, only six had served their apprenticeship outside Ludlow. All the rest had been trained in Ludlow, many of them by their own fathers or other relatives.

Glove making occurred throughout the town, with some concentration in Corve Street, the traditional centre of leather work. The apparatus of the trade would have been visible in many places, such as the drench tub below the Old Gate from which Ralph Harris lost five cattle skins in 1741, or pelts laid out to dry like the '23 leather skins' taken from John Jones's garden in Corve Street in 1784. Because much of the industry was home-based, gloving workplaces are now rare, but many of the fine houses built by prosperous glovers do survive, and are the industry's greatest legacy.

No. 30 Corve Street, built in 1749 by John Hoiser, glover. It was later the home of Samuel Acton, glover.

Cottages in Linney, converted from the ruined St Leonard's Chapel. Employees of Samuel Acton lived here.

'The lesser sort'

Many in this group were wage-earning journeymen and labourers in regular employment. The work of journeymen is sometimes referred to, as when a hat 'made by David Rowland, journeyman', was stolen in 1700. There were citizens such as 'one Tipton, an industrious working man', from whom £30 savings was stolen in 1774. The lives of women are often obscure, with court depositions giving rare glimpses, as

This detail from a painting of Lower Broad Street shows a group of what seem to be the poorer residents of Ludlow in the 1820s.

of Mary, wife of William Lane, labourer, who 'nursed for the parish' in 1724. A few labourers owned property, such as Edward Fewtrell, who had two houses in Corve Street in 1739; while Richard Pugh had £50 'ready money' when he died in 1728.

At the base of the social hierarchy were 'the poor', among them Thomas Abley in one of the squatter settlements at Rock Lane. Charged with Hearth Tax in 1680, he protested that he had never paid anything to Church or poor as he had been 'by reason of his poverty always excused'. Many elderly and infirm poor were accommodated in the Almshouses, but others were helped by bequests, like that of Richard Davies, ironmonger, who in 1701 left £100 to be invested 'for eight poor widows'. The scale of the problem in times of crisis is shown by a list of paupers in 1817, which names 199 persons receiving out relief with another 32 in the Poor House. The list is a sad chronicle of human misery. Eight persons were lame, two were blind and 17 were ill in other ways, while one had an insane son. Three were wives whose husbands had been transported. There were many split homes, with 22 children living only with their mother and another 34 boarded out.

Some temporary residents were removed as vagrants, like John Renshaw, mason, to Liverpool in 1767. Travellers were often in trouble, as when William Powell of Bristol stole a coat from Lady Lloyd's stable in 1724. Army deserters were sometimes apprehended, such as Thomas Keppel of Leicestershire in 1778, from a regiment bound for Ireland.

This unknown woman, drawing water from the conduit at the Tolsey, is the kind of person that historical records rarely illuminate.

Markets and fairs

Monday continued to be market day. Blome writing in Britannia in 1673 declared that Ludlow was 'a very great market for corn, cattle and provisions'. There were then four annual fairs, and a fifth, on the Tuesday before Easter, was added in 1685. Tolls were paid at these fairs but in 1769 a toll-free fair on the Monday before Candlemass was promoted by the attorney Thomas Blainey. In 1822 the ancient May Fair was revived as another toll-free event at the instigation of Henry Wellings, who was later carried round town in a chair decorated with laurel. Further competition to the chartered fairs came from sales in villages, such as the '200 prime Leicester Sheep' at Bromfield on 27 September, 1825, a Ludlow fair day.

As the zeal for 'improvement' spread, attempts were made to locate animal standings so that a way was clear for the growing amount of wheeled traffic. In 1713 it was decreed that any person 'putting his cattle in the middle of the street shall pay for every head 10d'. Cattle were still concentrated in the Bull Ring, with sheep in Corve Street and pigs at the top of Old Street, where in 1806 The Golden Lion (now the Library) was described as 'in the Pig Market'. The horse fairs, in contrast, had more spacious quarters in Castle Square, with vendors and buyers coming from central Wales and many parts of the West Midlands. Corn was sold at the Market House, as were other goods, such as the silk handkerchiefs stolen from the stall of John Walsh, draper, in 1720. In 1739 the Shambles were cleared from the top of Mill Street, but within a few years a hop market had opened further down the street, outside what is now the Blue Boar.

Court records give glimpses of the people who came to town on market and fair days, making Ludlow a busy, bustling place. In 1674 Elizabeth Pearce of Stokesay was 'in the Market Cross selling cheese'. In 1691 Philip Bevan of Glaustrie in Radnorshire came to sell stockings. In 1727 John Watkins of Worcester sold cloth, but was accused of 'using a yard under measure'. Many came to sell and buy animals, such as Edward Dickson, a butcher and grazier from Bishops Castle, in 1758, while others sold a range of hardware goods, such as John Milner of Bridgnorth in 1809. Much drinking went on in Ludlow alehouses, and crime was commonplace, so that Mary Jones (1809-1906), recalling her Ludlow childhood, remembered that the Town Crier would make a proclamation warning against thieves.

Communications and Inns

Two of the routes designated 'Principal Roads' in Ogilby's Britannia of 1675 converged near Ludlow: the road from Worcester to Montgomery and that from Bristol to Chester. The 1686 census of stables at inns - a useful index of horse movement and therefore of the amount of road transport - recorded 173 at Ludlow, behind several towns in the north of Shropshire, but well ahead of anywhere in Herefordshire, including the county town. The journey from London was slow: pictures sent by the Ludlow carrier to Oakly Park in July 1684 were expected 'this day seventide'. Travel around Ludlow was notoriously difficult, especially in north Herefordshire, where as late as 1789 the Cambridge don Henry Gunning found the roads 'literally impassable after the autumn rains'.

Roads improved during the eighteenth century, which has been called 'the age of turnpike mania', turnpikes being the spiked gates where tolls were levied to pay for better maintenance. The network grew slowly at first but accelerated in the 1750s, when the lst. and 2nd. Ludlow Turnpike Trusts, in 1751 and 1756, brought improvements to roads radiating from Ludlow. The turnpikes helped the development of public coach services. These operated from London to Shrewsbury and Worcester by 1690 and to Hereford by 1722, but there is no record of a service to Ludlow before 1763. From this date a coach ran regularly between Ludlow and London via Worcester. In 1779 it left the Red Lion, on the corner of Market Street and Raven Lane, at 6 a.m. Tuesday, reaching London 'early the next day'. By 1794 there were four coaches a week from Ludlow inns, the fastest taking 24 hours. Services between

Detail from a picture of Lower Broad Street in the 1820s, showing four horses and a coach heading for Broad Gate. Mary Sneade recalled from her childhood the 'thrilling sound of post horns' as the mail 'mounted the steep street', though in 1792-94 the news it brought of atrocities in France 'was so often unbelievably horrible'.

Shrewsbury and Hereford were more sporadic but a 'New Post' was running by 1801. Thereafter services grew rapidly and by 1828 there were 27 coaches in and out of Ludlow a week.

The carrying trade also became more efficient, though carriers' wagons were much slower than coaches. A number of carriers worked the route to London, including the Wellings family. In the 1790s the advertised time was five and a half days. In 1782 a regu-

lar service between Hereford and Manchester was started, with the claim that previous carriers 'had not been regular in forwarding goods beyond Shrewsbury'. A network of local services also developed, with 26 weekly waggons or carts leaving Ludlow by 1826. This was also the age of canals, but the nearest was the Stourport to Leominster Canal, which in 1794 reached Woofferton, three miles south of Ludlow. It was proposed to link it to the Severn near Montgomery, to following the Teme valley and bisecting Lower Broad Street, but it was too expensive.

The waggon on this 1801 painting is probably that of John Taylor. It left his Corve Street warehouse early on Monday reaching The George, Smithfield, London 'about noon on Saturday'.

The inns were the nodal points of the transport sytem. The Crown and The Angel, facing each other across Broad Street, became the leading coaching inns. Vehicles could be hired, as from Joseph Farrar at The Angel in 1782, who advertised 'neat post chaises, able horses and careful drivers'. Accommodation for horses was an important facility for inns, the landlord of The Feathers announcing in 1824 that: 'The excellent Stabling of this Inn will be carefully attended to by one experienced, civil and steady ostler'. Many of the country carriers loaded and put down at some of the smaller inns, as at The Compasses for Bishop's Castle in the 1830s.

The town's 'commodious inns' and its smaller alehouses provided drink and food for local people and for the crowds at markets and fairs, as well as for travellers. In 1745 there were 49 licensed premises in Ludlow, increasing to 55 by 1792, though there was some contraction later. Meetings, commercial transactions, political gatherings and auctions were often held in inns, and entertainments were organised, such as the 'Great Cock-Match' at The Eagle and Child in 1731. The leading innkeepers often had high inventory values, the goods of Thomas Hitchcott of The Bear, for example, being worth £550; but these were not as high as at least three contemporary innkeepers' inventories in the north and east of Shropshire, on more frequented routes, all of which were over £700.

The Corporation and their buildings

The composition of the Corporation changed during these years, largely due to greater participation by the land-owning gentry. This was a feature of many towns, Beverley and Warwick being examples, but it did not occur everywhere. Bridgnorth, for example, was governed almost exclusively by tradesmen. At Ludlow, 133 of the 298 members between 1660 and 1835 were gentry. Fifteen were Herberts and Clives of Oakly Park and their relations, but other local families were represented through several generations, including six Baldwyns of Corvedale or Stokesay, six Salweys of Richard's Castle and four Charltons of Ludford.

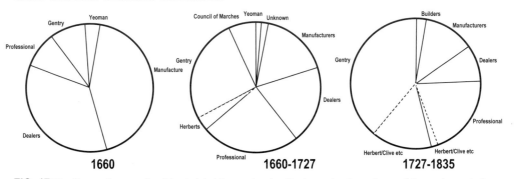

FIG. 17 The Corporation membership at stated times, showing the increasing importance of the gentry and of the Herberts and Clives. Their control of Ludlow's parliamentary representation dates from 1727.

Men from all social groups served as High Bailiff and held other offices, but manufacturers, dealers and professional men took more than their proportionate share, among them Richard Davies, apothecary, a member from 1636 to 1683, and High Bailiff four times. The number of annual meetings declined, from more than ten a year before 1700 to an average of barely two after 1800. To some degree, however, this was because of delegation to committees, individuals and the Town Clerk. Attendances, recorded from 1753, show great variety. Men like Samuel Monger, glover, William Russell, mercer, and Somerset Davies, attorney, all served for more than 40 years and attended 90% or more of the meetings. Such men were the work-horses of the Corporation. Men like Richard Salwey, with 15 attendances out of 44, saw the Corporation as a gentlemen's club, to be attended when convenient, while in other cases attendance was abysmal, as with John Smyth of Stoke Court, Burford, who came once in 32 years.

The practice of keeping four sets of accounts, not all covering the same period, makes it difficult to analyse the Corporation's finances. Income from rents – £573 in 1734-35, nearly £3,000 in 1831-32 – was enough to meet regular responsibilities: the salaries of employees, payments to the almspeople and maintenance of streets and public services. Major building projects were often timed when tenants paid large fines when taking new leases, but borrowing, sometimes from the Corporation's own members, was often necessary, part of the 'hand to mouth' system of small town finance at this time. Expenditure on entertaining included the provision of beer, coals and gunpowder at times of national rejoicing, as at coronations or after naval and military victories. Other sums went to enhance the Corporation's image and therefore its authority: repair of the maces, gowns for Aldermen and Councillors, uniforms for the beadles and Town Crier.

Some credit for 'improving' Ludlow and leaving a fine legacy of Georgian architecture should go to the Corporation. Each year twelve members were appointed surveyors, to control encroachments and other aspects of building. In 1704, for example, William Pearce was allowed to erect a stone wall at the Tolsey 'so far as the Getty [jetty] doth extend'. By employing architects like William Baker and T.F. Pritchard, the Corporation encouraged good design, and their employment on private houses often stemmed from contacts first made through the Corporation.

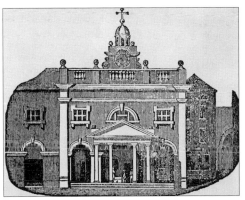

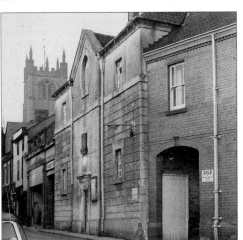

Above left: The Butter Cross, built 1743–46 in a classical style 'with just a touch of the Baroque' to replace the New House at a cost of nearly £1,000. The architect was William Baker of Audlam, a gentleman-farmer. Above: Hosier's Almshouses, rebuilt 1758-59 at a cost of over £1200, is an imposing building, with the Ludlow arms in its pediment. It was surveyed and supervised by Thomas Farnolls Pritchard of Shrewsbury. Left: The gaol in Tower Street, rebuilt 1764-65 at a cost of £422. The tablet was inscribed: the Common Prison of this Town in place of Galdeford's Tower, an ancient Prison and Gate.

Herberts, Clives and the parliamentary representation of Ludlow

A seat in the House of Commons - which brought prestige and power - was a widespread aspiration, and from 1660 to 1727 there was intense competition for the two Ludlow seats. The successful candidates from 21 elections came from 12 local families and three outsiders, among them the Herberts of Oakly Park, Bromfield. After 1727, members of this family and their relatives the Clives held both seats until 1832, in person or through supporters.

The senior members of the vast Herbert family were Dukes of Beaufort and Earls of Pembroke, but the Herberts of Bromfield, shown on the far right of the pedigree on page 125, were relatively poor and obscure. The lack of male issue to their cousins, the Herberts of Chirbury, meant, however, that greater status and wealth came to Francis Herbert (d.1718) by inheritance from his mother. His probate inventory has the astonishing valuation of more than £19,000, showing rents from central Ireland and many parts of Wales and Shropshire. This power base gave the Herberts the edge on other candidates and in 1727, from a franchise of over 800 freemen, many of them resident outside the borough, Francis's elder son, Henry Arthur Herbert, and his brother Richard secured both Ludlow seats by comfortable majorities.

The Herberts, and the Clives after them, had to work hard and invest heavily to retain their control. In 1754 it was alleged that H.A.Herbert, then Lord Powis, had spent 'twenty to thirty thousand pounds' to secure the seats. The marriage of his daughter, Henrietta, to Edward Clive, son of Robert Clive of India, was a brilliant match for both parties, replenishing the Herberts' fortune, and eventually bringing Edward Clive the Earldom which had eluded his father. It ensured too that Ludlow would remain a pocket borough to 1832, in spite of mounting opposition and the personal unpopularity of the new Earl of Powis, who was known for his 'monstrous extravagance'.

There had always been some opposition to the Herberts, but this grew as the national clamour for Reform gathered pace. The leaders locally were tradesmen and lawyers and the printer and bookseller William Felton, who was remembered as 'a strenuous supporter of Civil and Religious Liberty' on his parish church memorial. The headlines, however, were often taken by E.L. Charlton Esq. of Ludford, a maverick politician who forced an election in 1826, though he only secured two votes from a much reduced electorate.

124

FIG 18. A simplified pedigree of branches of the Herbert family, showing the recurring links between Powis Castle, Montgomeryshire, and Oakly Park, Bromfield

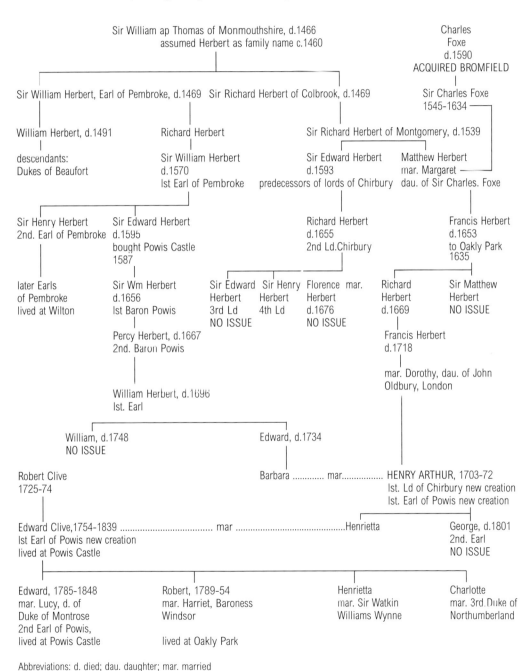

Abbreviations: d. died; dau. daughter; mar. married

Conformity and non-conformity

A census of adults in 1676 listed 1350 conformists, compared with 21 non-conformists and five 'papists'. Early in the 18th century, large numbers were worshipping at St Laurence's, there being 968 communicants over the Easter period in 1723, while 28 young persons were admitted to the sacrament. By 1795, however, confirmations only occurred every few years, and there are several contemporary reports of small congregations. The Church Wardens' Accounts show an on-going struggle to maintain the fabric but in 1750 new galleries were erected over the north and south aisles. All eight bells were re-cast in 1732 while a Snetzler organ - the core of the present fine instrument - was donated by Lord Powis in 1764. The restoration by the Corporation of the huge east window in 1830 was the first of a series of 19th century measures to enhance St Laurence's.

The non-conformists of 1676 were Anabaptists, but after 1700 the largest group were Independents. They travelled to services in Leominster, an early centre of non-conformity, but later they met at what is now No.16 High Street. There they were assailed by the mob in 1731, but when the Bailiffs refused to enforce redress, supporters in London came to their aid, causing a small chapel to be built in lower Corve Street in 1735. There is a tradition that 'even women aided in the work by carrying stones in their aprons'. The church had variable fortunes, but thrived at times, as under the Rev. David Francis, 1800-24, who started the town's first Sunday School. By 1830 the Independents - later called Congregationalists - were able to build a new chapel in Old Street, now a private house.

The 'evangelical awakening' of the mid-18th century, did not reach Ludlow for many years, though Charles Wesley came to Ludlow to court his future wife, a member of the Gwynn family of Breconshire who often resided in the town. The Methodists were first established on Clee Hill but a chapel was built in Lower Broad Street in 1800, with a congregation of 'about 300' by 1832. There were also Primitive Methodists from 1822, who met in private houses.

The interior of the lower Corve Street chapel in 1910, showing the 18th century pews and pulpit decorated for harvest festival. It was sold in 1830 and demolished in the 1950s.

Education and Culture

Like other 'fashionable' towns, Ludlow had a reputation for boarding education, being listed in England's Gazetteer of 1751 for 'the education of Welsh youth of both sexes'. Headmasters of the Grammar School added to their income by taking boarders, some of them eminent later. There were private schools for day boys and boarders, such as that of Charles Tyler, writing master (d.1710), in Dinham, and of Thomas Whittington (d. 1763), mathematician, at 40 Broad Street. A typical girls' school was that of Mrs Holloway (d.1792), at 53 Broad Street, who charged boarders eleven guineas a year for 'Needlework, Morals and Polite Behaviour', with special masters for 'dancing, French and music if required'.

For the children of the poor, a Blue Coat Charity School was founded at the Guildhall in 1714. There were 50 boys and 30 girls, aged six to ten, many of them going on to pauper apprenticeships. This school, much declined, later transferred to the Workhouse in Old Street but in 1785 it was re-established over the Butter Cross, with 45 pupils. In 1813 it was absorbed in a much larger Church of England National School and by 1820 there were 170 boys enrolled above the Butter Cross and 138 girls at a new building in Brand Lane, though attendance was not good. A number of small 'dame schools' also provided basic education for small fees, e.g. that of Ann Hickman, mantua-maker, of Raven Lane from 1787 to 1793. In totality, however, many people still lacked even the rudiments of education, with the number of people able to sign their names on marriage certificates being only 70% for males and 53% for females in the 1820s.

In the upper echelons, high educational standards were often reached, with several people of learning living in or near Ludlow, for example R.P.Knight (1750-1824), numismatist and classical scholar. Books are listed in 20% of Ludlow inventories between 1660 and 1745, while early nineteenth century sale notices often include books, e.g. the 'extensive and valuable library of books of the first class in superb bindings' on offer at a Broad Street house in 1821. In contrast, south Shropshire was known for superstition and old customs. As in Hardy's Wessex, the sale of a wife was accepted as an alternative to divorce, as at Ludlow market in 1814, when John Hall sold his wife by public auction for 2s 6d., 'conformable to an ancient law'.

A consensus of good taste

The fashion for brick and symmetrical facades, rare in earlier periods, came suddenly to Ludlow about 1680. There were ambitious plans to improve the town, such as the proposal by William Gower, formerly M.P., made in writing to Robert Harley in 1704, to replace the 'neglected buildings' of the castle by 'a handsome square'. Nothing came of this, but in 1714, as he rode up Broad Street, John Macky noted 'Handsome houses, Sash-windowed on each Side'. Changes in house plans came more slowly, the first known central hall and staircase being that of 14 Castle Street in 1728. Rebuilding and refronting continued intermittently until 1832, with phases of building, as in the years after 1763, showing some correlation with known cycles of national construction and investment.

Most Ludlow houses were built by teams of master craftsmen, each employing labourers, sometimes on a part-time basis. A contract was made in 1703 between John Salwey and Charles Woodall, carpenter, Thomas Hattam and John Waties, masons, to rebuild 17 Broad Street at a cost of £59 15s., though the materials were paid for separately. They were all members of dynasties of builders which, with others such as the Steads after 1800, were active in Ludlow over many generations. Specialist craftsmen were often drafted in, as was William Piper, plasterer, at the Broad Gate in 1696, who was paid 10d a day 'to sile [seal] walls and plaster with lime and mortar' in various rooms. The craftsmen used the pattern books of the time for their detail, though solecisms and irregularities often occurred, such as the eight Venetian windows at 38 Broad Street of about 1770 - famously cited by Alec Clifton Taylor as 'over-egging the pudding'. In some houses architects were involved, but hints of work in the town by Thomas White of Worcester (d.1748) and Michael Sidnell of Bristol (d.after 1745) have yet to be corroborated.

In highly regarded articles in Country Life in 1945/46, Christopher Hussey has eulogised Ludlow's 'architectural sequences', noting the way in which buildings relate to each other and adjust to the slopes on which many of them are built. The same point underlies much of the statutory listing which has taken place in recent years , which includes buildings for 'group value', as well as for intrinsic merit. 'The architectural distinction maintained is remarkable', Hussey tell us, 'well into the nineteenth century'.

Nos 35-38 Broad Street, which took on their present form in the mid-18th century. Hussey notes: So far as is possible, eaves, lintels and sill levels are carried through by the nearest corresponding feature on the next house above.

This late Georgian arcade in King Street, which probably replaced an earlier jettied building, relates well to the different architectural styles included in this view, another quality of the Ludlow townscape which is praised by Hussey.

A selection from more than a hundred Georgian doorways in Ludlow, showing changing taste over sixty years.

55 Mill Street, 1740: rather heavy fluted pilasters carry capitals and flat hood, with rectangular overlight. Part of a terrace of houses for letting.

14 Corve Street, 1770: ornate broken pediment with tracery, a replica of a 1750 doorway in Westminster, probably from the same pattern book.

Dinham Lodge, c.1800, a more delicate design, with slim fluted columns and an ornamental fanlight: a fashionable replacement for an older design.

Lower income housing

Especially from the 1760s, when the town's population began to increase, many small houses were built in Ludlow. The groupings were shaped by the medieval burgage plots, often with houses behind earlier street frontages. This process is known as back-building and was a feature of many historic towns. In Ludlow the arrangements within the plots were often loose and informal, suggesting sporadic growth rather than a single development. In some places, however, especially on the east side of Old Street, more regular layouts occurred, reminiscent of back-building in crowded cities such as Nottingham. The owners were usually artisans, innkeepers or small scale tradesmen, who financed their projects by loans, often from farmers in the surrounding countryside, and repaid them from the rents of tenants. These developments were mostly in the less fashionable, eastern parts of the town, or at the bottom of the grander residential streets. Of those recieving relief as paupers in 1817, 45 lived in Lower or Upper Galdeford, 19 in Old Street. 15 in Lower Broad Street, 14 in Corve Street and 11 in Holdgate Fee, compared to only four in Dinham, three in Broad Street and none at all in Mill Street or Castle Street.

FIG 20 This extract shows Dean's Yard (D) and Noakes's Yard (N), two congested burgages on the east side of Old Street. Dean's Yard was developed after 1793 by John Dean, an innkeeper who kept The Seven Stars at the front of the plot; and Noakes Yard after 1800 by James Noakes, who had a baker's shop in Broad Street.

FIG 19 (Left) This 1885 O. S. map of part of Upper Galdeford has a large plot on the left, once the property of the Sherman family. There were six houses, a stable and a workshop here in 1783, when the owner was Benjamin Beach, brickmaker. In 1798 the narrow plot to the east, once a lane to the Town Barn, and the plot next to it, were owned by Thomas Meredith, wheelwright, who borrowed money for building from Thomas Tomkins of Aldon, yeoman.

CHAPTER EIGHT

1832-1901: THE YEARS AFTER REFORM

Clivites and Reformers

The Reform Bill was carried in 1832, after fifteen months of political agitation unparallelled in the history of Great Britain. Ludlow was one of the old parliamentary boroughs which retained two seats. Others were reduced to one, while Bishop's Castle, a notoriously 'rotten borough', was one of 56 which were totally disenfranchised. Many new seats were created, two of them for Shropshire, which now had north and south Parliamentary Divisions. The new system, with the vote going to £10 householders in the boroughs and to forty shilling freeholders in the counties, was more representative than previously, but it was far short of what the radicals had wanted. There were adjustments in 1867, when the franchise was widened and many boroughs, including Ludlow, were reduced to one member; and again in 1885, when Ludlow ceased to return its own member and became part of the Ludlow division of Shropshire, which had one member.

The early years brought political turbulence, as the Clives struggled to keep their control of Ludlow. 'We have no Tories or Radicals,' it was later observed, 'but Clivites and Reformers'. The Clives began their campaign on 25 September 1832, when a cavalcade 'more than a mile in length', with 'upwards of 40 carriages' and 'an immense concourse of horsemen' met at the Old Field to escort into Ludlow the sitting members: Lord Edward Clive, heir to the Earl of Powis, and his brother R.H. Clive of Oakly Park. The electorate, of 359 voters, returned Lord Clive, but showed their independence by bringing in Edward Romilly, a Whig from south Wales, as the second member. This was at the expense of R.H. Clive, who in pique vowed never to stand for Ludlow again. Later elections were yet more vitriolic, especially that of 1839 to choose one member to replace Edward Clive when he became Earl of Powis. There were allegations of bribery and treating on both sides, causing the election to be declared void. For the Clivites, John Frail came from Shrewsbury 'to manage the dirty work', while both sides offered three-figure sums for individual votes. Beriah Botfield of Hopton Court, whose wealth came from iron, took up the Conservative mantle in 1840 and 1841, but from 1847 until 1885 the Clives re-asserted themselves, taking one of the Ludlow seats until 1865 and the single seat until 1885.

An elected Borough Council

The growing unpopularity of oligarchic corporations, such as Ludlow's Twelve and Twenty Five, was one of the reasons for the pressure for Reform. Opposition to the Ludlow Corporation built up over many years, led by a number of tradesmen, the lawyer George Anderson and the bookseller and printer William Felton. Their cause célèbre was St Leonard's Chapel, trusteeship of which had been acquired by the Corporation in 1771. The chapel was in poor condition but instead of carrying out repairs, the Corporation demolished it, using the stones to rebuild Corve Bridge, and leased the site to one of their own members, Samuel Acton, who built glovers' work-shops and cottages there. In 1813, when there was concern about St Laurence's churchyard, with burials causing 'indecent disturbance of bodies', the matter was taken up by the Reformers, who argued that St Leonard's Chapel and churchyard should be brought back into public use. The case eventually went to the Vice-Chancellor's Court in London, where the Corporation was found guilty of 'a gross breach of trust', though the order to rebuild the chapel was evaded for many years.

The Municipal Corporations Act of 1835 laid down that the Corporation should be replaced by a Borough Council of 12 Councillors, elected by the adult male ratepayers, and four Aldermen, elected by the new Councillors. In a poll on 26 December 1835 all twelve seats were taken by the Reformers: eight tradesmen, three surgeons and a schoolmaster, with votes ranging from 170 to 153, compared with 87 to 67 for the Tories, four of whom had been members of the Corporation. The Council had its first meeting on 31 December 1835 to elect four fellow Reformers as Aldermen, and on 1 January 1836 one of these, William Edwards draper – a campaigner for Reform since 1813 or earlier – was elected Mayor.

The hand-over of office was acrimonious and protracted. In June 1836 the Council applied for a Writ to compel the former Bailiffs to surrender documents, and in 1837 the Town Clerk went to London to pursue the matter in the Court of Chancery. For some months, also, the use of the Guildhall was disputed, each side putting men to eat and sleep there to maintain their rights. At first the mood was violent, but the old Corporation representative, Wiliam Pyefinch, later admitted that 'the fierce spirit of animosity soon quits the martial bosoms of the garrison when they ... eat and drink together', and testified that by May Fair day 1836 'the citadel was deserted by all but myself'.

The Charity Estates: the Great Law Suit

A fierce and sometimes bitter mood persisted in Ludlow politics for some years. The Reformers - now styled Radicals - dominated the Borough Council until 1843, but the Conservatives then began ten years of control, with three former members of the pre-Reform Corporation as successive mayors. There were several reasons for the Radicals' demise, but the prime one was a protracted law suit over the disposition of the Charity estates.

The Municipal Corporation Act insisted that charity and municipal property should be separated. In 1837 officers of the Lord Chancellor appointed 17 Ludlow Municipal Charity Trustees, nine of whom were Radicals and seven Conservatives . The Trustees were to be responsible for the charities inherited from the Palmer's Guild - which included the Grammar School, Hosier's Almshouses and the stipends of Preacher and Reader. Initially, it was agreed that lands which would raise some £540 a year should be transferred to the Trustees, that being the sum spent on the charities in 1835.

Such a figure, about a fifth of the Corporation's expenditure, was blatantly unfair to the charities, for the Palmers' Guild lands constituted some three-quarters of the Corporation estate. Seeing this as a stick with which to beat the Radicals, and as a means to gain popularity with the electorate, the Clives were the first to propose a better deal for the Charities. Later, a compromise of £850 a year was agreed, and in 1841 William Downes, the Radical Town Clerk, went to London to promote a Parliamentary bill for such an outcome.

At this point, two Ludlow petitioners objected to the compromise: E T Charlton, a compulsive disputant who had grudges against both the Clives and the Council, and Revd Arthur Willis, Headmaster of Ludlow Grammar School since 1838. Willis, 'a man of high principle', had been a Housemaster at Shrewsbury School and had visions of expanding Ludlow Grammar School if the charities could provide more funds, including the granting of university exhibitions. Their protest plunged the town into five years of venomous litigation. In London courts, the petitioners argued that if the true value of the lands had been realised since 1552, the Charities would have benefited by £184,249, but they admitted that recovery of such a sum was impracticable, and therefore settled for £1,525 a year, which doubled the existing expenditure on most items and added £200 a year for exhibitions.

An Act of Parliament confirming these arrangements was passed on 7 May 1846. Lands in 16 parishes, including ten farms, were made over to the Trustees to yield £1,525 a year. The Borough Council had to give the Trustees £4,305 for repairs, which had been greviously neglected, and were obliged to meet all legal costs, which totalled £37,000 - and which they could meet only by selling nearly all their Ludlow properties. The town was not bankrupt after the great law suit, as was sometimes alleged, but it was greatly impoverished.

E. L. Charlton died in 1845 but Willis was left to face the town's wrath. Town boys were withdrawn from the school; ill-feeling between Willis's boys, mostly boarders, and those of his usher were such that a stone partition had to be built in the schoolroom; his salary was with-held from 1846 until 1850; and a silly dispute about school times, where Willis himself showed pedantry and lack of tact, led to notice of dismissal in 1850. His appeal to the Master of the Rolls was upheld, but by then Willis was a sick man, and he died in July 1851, aged only 47, causing Sir Rowland Hill (of Penny Post fame), who had acted for the Petitioners in front of the Lord Chancellor, to remark:

Wiliam Harding, grocer, Alderman from 1836 and Mayor of Ludlow 1838-39.

'I knew the case on both sides and a more cruel case of oppression I never met with. The man did great service and his ruin followed directly from the service which he rendered.'

The Borough Council to 1901

Politics continued to be sharply contested in Ludlow for some years, with the Radicals regaining power in 1853. Later in the century, however, the great issues of national debate found little echo at Ludlow, and much of the heat went out of local affairs. Most councillors were leading businessmen or from the professions. It was an honour to be on the Council and the office of Mayor was prestigious. John Williams, solicitor, was Town Clerk from 1843 to 1880 and was succeeded by his son, John Herbert Williams. The Council became more professional in its conduct of business as the

George Cocking, chemist, who married Harding's daughter; Mayor 1860-61.

century progressed. In 1836 they appointed Thomas Pritchard, a Corve Street maltster, to be Treasurer at £25 a year, but by 1895 they were employing Thomas Atherden, banker. At first, technical advice was obtained through contract, but a Borough Surveyor was in post by 1879. There was a Superintendent of Police by 1861, with three other officers, a Captain of the Fire Engine, and a host of lesser officials, such as the Keeper of the Waterworks in Lower Mill Street. Much of the expenditure was on public amenities, an echo of the Civic Gospel then current in Birmingham, where public libraries, sewage disposal plants, and gas lighting were provided with evangelical fervour. One costly item was the building of new sewers, as mapped by T.Curley, C.E., F.G.S., in 1862. Other services were provided by public companies, including a new gasworks at Temeside, replacing works opened in Upper Galdeford in 1822. The Council eventually procured the silver plate of the old Corporation and employed a Common Sergeant and a Mace Bearer to carry the three maces.

Another fashion was for new, ostentatious town halls, and in 1887, after much debate, the Council decided to demolish the old market hall and build a successor to mark the Queen's Golden Jubilee in that year. The project, which cost over £6,000, necessitated a loan which was not paid off until the 1930's. The building, designed by Henry Cheers of Twickenham, aroused great local pride and was opened with a civic banquet in 1889.

The Town Hall, sometimes known as The Corn Exchange, in 1892. There was a covered market on the ground floor, an assembly hall above, and a handsome Council chamber overlooking Castle Street. The architectural style, 'of curly stone and virulent brick', was admired in the 1890s but later became unfashionable.

Social and occupational structure in 1841

The availability of decennial census returns from 1841 onwards makes it possible to reconstruct Ludlow society in a way not possible for earlier periods. The 1841 census gives a particularly useful picture of the town in its twilight years as a fashionable social centre. The charts below show that 41% of the population were in employment, and that of these, 30.8% were in service. These figures are comparable with those for other market towns, such as Banbury and Melton Mowbray. Fig 22 gives the figures for each group and in most cases for the major classes of employment within those groups.

The figures reveal a mixed economy, with manufacturing and service the principal activities. The numbers in agriculture suggest that food was still being produced locally, much of it on the town fields, now almost entirely enclosed. The building trades were healthy, with a number of prominent family firms such as the Russells of Old Street. Glove manufacture had declined, due to competition from abroad and areas of cheaper production, leaving the town without a staple industry - a fate common to many small towns at this time, for example Monmouth, once important for caps. But the industrial base was broad, with the clothing trades meeting much of the local need, though some of those employed, as in clothing, were retailers as well as manufacturers. Malting was more important than the figures suggest, for 20 of the maltsters had their own businesses - 13 of them in Corve Street - and probably employed general labourers. Most enterprises were small, but there were larger concerns on the edge of the town: Hodges' iron foundry at Castle Mills, Wade's paper works at Steventon and Evans' woollen manufactory in Lower Broad Street.

The numbers working in finance, including five accountants and three bankers, show a more sophisticated system than previously. They, with the town's lawyers, doctors, surgeons and auctioneers, illustrate Ludlow's continuing role as a service centre for a large rural area. More menial services had a largely local role, including 17 washerwomen, 13 laundresses and five chimney sweeps. In 1861 one sweep

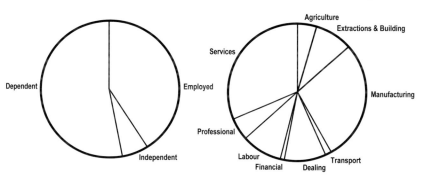

FIG 21

The left hand chart refers to the whole population which was 5,064 in 1841. The right hand chart shows the main occupational categories for the 2,054 people in employment.

FIG. 22 Occupational/social status groups in Ludlow, 1841
Group totals **A**   Class totals **B**

	A	B		A	B
AGRICULTURE			**TRANSPORT**		
labourers	73			18	18
gardeners	21		**DEALING**		
farmers	8		drapers/mercers	32	
others	4	106	food	61	
BUILDING			drink	55	
brickmakers	2		lodging house keepers	3	
builders	14		books/stationery	8	
carpenters/joiners	70		ironmongers/china	19	
masons/bricklayers	45		shopkeepers/hawkers	22	
plumbhers/glaziers	16		auctioneers,etc.	8	208
others	36	183	**FINANCE**		
MANUFACTURING				17	17
machinery/tools	11		**LABOUR**		
blacksmiths/founders	32			181	181
nailers	35		**PUBLIC SERVICE/PROFESSIONAL**		
non-ferrous metals	20		local services	15	
leather/chandlers	14		lawyers	15	
wood/furniture	46		medical	31	
saddlers/wheelwrights	20		arts	9	
coach makers	4		teachers	22	
paper	14		clergy	12	
cloth/flax	25		armed services	8	112
clothes (glovers 32)	290		**SERVICE**		
bakers/millers	45		men	86	
maltsters	24		female	493	
watch-makers	7		cleaners/barbers	54	633
printers/bindresses	9	596	**INDEPENDENT**		
			gentry	55	
			others	222	277
			DEPENDENT	45	45

The bill-head of John Smith, brazier, pewterer, ironmonger, and tin-plate worker in King Street in the 1840s.

The open shop front of William Evans, butcher, at what is now 15 Bull Ring; sketched in 1846.

An advertisement of William Kinnersley, who traded from 1844 into the 1850s.

employed two 'lads', including his grandson, aged ten: shades of The Water-Babies indeed! The 181 labourers were another major social group, some of them living in cheap lodging houses, such as that of Jane Powell in Holdgate Fee, an 89 year old widow who had 24 persons under her roof!

Of the 277 persons classed as independent, many were elderly, living with working sons or daughters, but 55 were heads of households living off income from land or invested capital. A few were retired people of distinction like Sir Edward Thomason, a Birmingham manufacturer who rented what is now High Hall. The majority, however, were of local origins, with a range of backgrounds. About 15 were members of what can be called 'lesser gentry' families. Eleven had links with the professions – including the three Meyricke sisters of Dinham Lodge, whose brother was Reader of Ludlow – and 14 were retired tradesmen or tradesmens' widows. The presence of such families shows that Ludlow was still something of a fashionable social and cultural centre, as do some facets of the occupational structure – a coach building firm, the number of cabinet makers, watch-makers, printers, booksellers and stationers, artists (four) and musicians. Its best days, however, were clearly over - and it is indicative that the only great landowner to have a house in Ludlow was Viscount Boyne – and he visited it only rarely.

The new Assembly Rooms

The post-Reform years brought many innovations to Ludlow, among them the new Assembly Rooms. The motivator seems to have been Sir Edward Thomason, who addressed a public meeting on 22 December 1837, chaired by Lord Clive. Plans, drawn up by Messrs. Stead and Son, architects, were submitted for two buildings at the top of Mill Street: a museum for Ludlow's Natural History Society, founded in 1833; and Assembly Rooms containing a 'principal room for balls, concerts and lectures', supper room and card room. Shareholders were invited and a committee set up of gentry and Ludlow residents – but no members of the Borough Council! By February 1838 £6,200 had been raised and a pamphlet issued which began:

While neighbouring municipalities of very inferior pretensions are busily engaged in raising up Public Institutions for the ornament of their Town it is to be regretted that the Town of Ludlow has not so promptly exhibited those resources on this occasion which it has done in former times.

LUDLOW FESTIVAL.

RESPECTFULLY inform the Public, that their MUSICAL FESTIVAL will take place on FRIDAY, Nov. 6th, when a SELECTION OF SACRED MUSIC Will be performed in the CHURCH of ST. LAWRENCE, in the Morning.

AND IN THE EVENING, A GRAND MISCELLANEOUS CONCERT Will take place in the NEW ASSEMBLY ROOMS of the New Buildings.

PRINCIPAL VOCALISTS, MISS BIRCH, MISS A. WILLIAMS, MISS M. WILLIAMS, MR. HOBBS, AND MR. J. WILLIAMS. PRINCIPAL INSTRUMENTAL PERFORMERS, MR. BLAGROVE, MR. LINDLEY, MR. W. WILLIAMS, AND MR. REE. An efficient number of Chorus Singers have been engaged for the occasion.

MR. REE AND THE MISSES WILLIAMS

Top: An early event – The first Ludlow Festival! Above: Assembly Rooms in 1887.

The buildings were opened on 2 July 1840, when they were the venue for Ludlow Race Ball, a highlight of the social season. An even grander occasion was on 17 December, the sycophantic Salopian Journal reporting:

The first Ludlow Winter Assembly took place in the New Room on Thursday evening and was most brilliantly and fashionably attended, including upwards of 130 of the elite and fashion of the town and neighbourhood and all the principal branches of the noble house of Powis.

Ironically, this amenity came when Ludlow's social reputation was waning. Events became less glamorous, and the building was something of a white elephant. In 1899 the shareholders offered the building to the Town Council for a free library and educational purposes at the bargain price of £1,500. But the offer was rejected as 'an inexpedient' use of public money, to the indignation of The Ludlow Advertiser, which lamented: 'The voting of certain members of the Town Council have ceased to surprise us'.

The Union Workhouse

Another new building was the Workhouse on Gravel Hill. It opened in 1839 as a result of the Poor Law Amendment Act of 1834, one of a series of grim institutions built all over the country for groups or unions of parishes. The Ludlow Workhouse served 38 parishes centred on Ludlow and could accommodate some 300 inmates, though there were rarely more than 200. In 1850 about 60 of these came from Ludlow. Workhouses were administered by elected Guardians, and those at Ludlow were largely land-owning gentry like Sir Charles Cuyler of Henley Hall, clergy and other professional men.

The aim of the Workhouse was deterrence. It was a harsh system, designed to make life as unattractive as possible for the undeserving poor. 'The workhouse should be like a cold bath', proclaimed Edwin Chadwick, a civil servant, 'unpleasant in contemplation, but invigorating in its effects'. The sexes and age groups were strictly segregated. The daily regime, controlled by bells, was monotonous and regimented. Food was sparse, with bread and cheese always for supper, and meat only on Tuesdays. Work was hard and tedious, usually stone breaking for able bodied men, and opium picking for women. Discipline was enforced by a range of punishments. Staff were poorly trained and often incompetent. One Master, David Shut was dismissed in 1855 after being intoxicated for 24 days, though his successor, William Harris, a strict disciplinarian, survived for seven years. Many inmates were women, including widows, deserted wives and unmarried mothers; and the proportion of children in the Ludlow workhouse was high.

The Ludlow Workhouse followed a common plan, not unlike that used for the County Gaol at Shrewsbury in 1797. In both cases, the purpose was to control recalcitrant inmates. The building was designed by Matthew Stead, but the cost, £6,750, was more than twice the estimate. Much of the building has been demolished, but the Administration block remains as part of Ludlow Hospital.

140

Social decline - but slow growth as a market town

The population, which was 5,064 in 1841, declined slightly by 1851, but rose during the second half of the century to 6,373 in 1901, though nearly a quarter of the residents lived in the new suburb of East Hamlet, which had been part of Stanton Lacy parish until that year. This rate of growth, about 20%, was much less than that for England and Wales as a whole, which was just over 50%, but it was comparable to that of other market towns on the Welsh border, such as Leominster and Whitchurch.

The figures mask a decline in Ludlow's role as a fashionable social centre. The American novelist Henry James wrote in 1883 of the town's 'Spacious, mildly-ornamented brick houses which look as if there had been more going on in them in the first decade of this century than there is in the present'.

A major cause of this decline was the improvement in communications, which allowed the kind of people who had once come to Ludlow for their pleasures to travel further afield. The railway reached Ludlow from Shrewsbury on 20 April 1852 though the extension to Hereford didn't open until December 1853. The timetables show that London was only eight hours travelling time from Ludlow. As the railway network grew, gentry could go to and from the capital directly to their country estates, as did guests of Jasper More M.P. arriving at Linley near Bishop's Castle 'by the evening train' in the 1870s. With fewer gentry patronising the town, Ludlow was less attractive for retirement, and most private residents listed in Kelly's Directories were now linked to local professional and farming families.

With its social role diminished, and its manufacturing restricted, Ludlow was largely reliant from the 1850s on its traditional role as a market town. A boost came with the removal of the livestock market to the Smithfield in Lower Galdeford on the site of the former Austin Friary. Such moves took place in many towns in the mid-nineteenth century, as at Shrewsbury in 1850. The new site was close to the railway but plans to construct sidings came to nothing. By 1885 a rival market, operated by George Morris, had been established in Corve Street, along part of Station Drive. Though smaller, proximity to the railway gave the new location an advantage. By 1900 the old Smithfield had closed, and Morris had merged with Marshall and Poole, who had marketing interests elsewhere.

In 1894 Ludlow was described as a market town: 'a weekly corn and provision market is held on Monday, a weekly provision market on Saturday, a fair for cattle, horses, etc. on the second Monday in each month and a hiring fair on 1 May'. Country people walked or rode into market, many of them by the carriers' carts which operated regularly to and from surrounding towns and villages, usually terminating at Ludlow pubs. In 1885 there were 47 departures a week, including 13 from the George, nine from the Globe, eight from the Portcullis, and seven from the Compasses. George Griffiths, a Bewdley corn merchant, remarked that the farmers 'were of a better sort than most', particularly those from Corvedale. They dined at their favourite inns, Griffiths observing that at the Elephant and Castle 'such a fine healthy set of tenants of the soil were seldom to be met with as at that table'.

It is not easy to assess the effect of the late nineteenth century agricultural depression on Ludlow. Barrie Trinder has concluded that Shropshire, with its many dairy and sheep farms, was less affected than more arable regions , but 'suffered as much as any

from a succession of wet seasons, foot and mouth epidemics and other disasters of the late 1870s and early 1880s'. The paucity of Victorian buildings in the historic core of Ludlow, it can be argued, reflects lack of prosperity; but the rash of building in the new suburbs shows that some capital was available. One firm that did flourish was Marston Brothers, who began as Bull Ring bakers, but expanded as corn, seed and flour merchants, building a huge warehouse near the station in the 1890s. Many other businesses had an agricultural orientation, such as E. Bluck and Co. at 141 Corve Street, 'agents for all kinds of agricultural implements' in 1900.

Details from Louise Rayner's picture of the Butter Cross in the 1870s: Above: a carrier's waggon leaving High Street. Below: a country woman sits on the pavement, with customers appraising her wares.

Victoria Terrace, Gravel Hill: four imposing houses built in the early 1880s.

A clerk, a signalman and a waggoner were among those who lived in these terraced houses in New Street in 1891.

Ornate private houses in Steventon, built in the 1890s with fine views across the Teme Valley.

The expansion north-eastwards into Stanton Lacy, which began before 1841, accelerated in the 1850s, taking advantage of the sale of Corporation lands. By 1862 Gravel Hill Terrace had been built, opposite the old gas works, and properties had been marked out on each side of Julian Road, some of them with houses in place. By 1879 this part of Ludlow had become a smart suburb, with nearly a quarter of the private residents listed in Kelly's Directory living in Gravel Hill, Julian Road or Castle View, a new development north of New Road. Many of the new residents were successful tradesmen wanting to live away from their businesses, some of whom built large, ornate houses.

Another development was at East Hamlet, where long terraces of small houses were built, of the kind commonplace in industrial towns. These were financed by Benjamin Weale, a speculative builder who came from north Shropshire before 1877. Many of the residents were artisans and several worked on the railway. Others were employed at the brickworks in Fishmore Road, operated by Thomas Greenwood, from a family of Westbury brickmakers. The Raven Inn, at East Hamlet corner before 1862, was a focus for the new suburb, which soon had a few shops and a school, opened in 1879. By 1901 more houses had been built, including some in Sandpits Road and Fishmore, and there were good quality terraces and houses in Steventon.

Shades of Godliness

It is perhaps a surprising fact that church attendance in Ludlow on Sunday, 30 March, 1851, the day of the Ecclesiastical Census, was much lower than the national average. The interpretation of the census is not easy, and all returns may not be reliable, but the discrepancy is such that this statement has to be true. The main reason must surely be, as the figures below indicate, the low attendance at the parish church, which had one Sunday service, compared with two or three at the other churches.

There is evidence that St Laurence's had been moribund for some time. Its situation worsened in 1841 when the Radical Borough Council recommended the appointment of Revd. John Philips, a Whig of 'ample patrimony' whose political views aroused some hostility. Ann Fay, in 1851, called him 'a miserably low churchman, who is so unpopular that the Dissenting chapels and the alehouses are full on

FIG 23

Attendance at church services 30 March 1851	Highest attendances at a single service	% of total highest attendances	Total attendances at all services	% of total of all attendances
St Laurence's Parish Church	210	20.7	261	12.9
Independent	120	11.8	388	19.3
Plymouth Brethren	42	4.1	69	3.4
Wesleyan Methodist	344	33.9	622	30.9
Primitive Methodist	300	29.5	670	33.3
TOTAL	**1016**		**2010**	
% of population	21.7		42.8	
% for Shrewsbury	36.8		78.1	
% nationally	35.0		61.0	

Sundays'. But it was Philips who masterminded the new National Schools building in Lower Galdeford, a scheme at which 'old Ludlow shook its head'. He was one of those, also, who promoted the Gilbert Scott restoration of St Laurence's in 1859-61, though there were complaints in The Shrewsbury Chronicle about 'taking down the noble galleries' and of 'a return to Popery!'

Philips' successor in 1867 was another autocrat, who married Lady Victoria Clive. In 1876 it was reported that the Rector, Revd. ffarington Clayton 'has immense influence' and is 'difficult to oppose', but these qualities did achieve things. In 1870 St Stephen's Chapel, a mission church, opened in Galdeford, then a poor area, while in 1881 St John's was built in the salubrious Gravel Hill suburb.

After a slow start, non-conformity spread quickly in Ludlow. The Wesleyan Chapel was extended in 1835; a new Primitive Methodist Chapel in Old Street opened in 1836; there were small congregations of Baptists and Plymouth Brethren; and in 1856 the Congregationalists opened a schoolroom. In 1862 the Baptists built a chapel in Rock Lane; while the Salvation Army opened their 'Barracks' in Lower Galdeford in 1888. Though much of the membership came from the poorer strata of society, all the churches had leaders of standing, such as chemist George Cocking, Mayor in 1860, 'a pillar' of the Congregational church.

The evangelistic fervour of Methodism, in particular, is caught in the letters of John Thar, Primitive Methodist Preacher. 'I am enjoying more of the Lord than I have for some time past' he wrote in 1843. The following year he reported: 'We have joined about 30 this quarter in Ludlow. Bless the Lord!' Some of those who opted for the alehouses must have been off-put by the high moral tone of Methodism, as in 1852, when their minister condemned sports on Castle Green as 'degrading, particularly the race by women'. But others flocked to the Word, and in 1867 a Schools' Commissioner reported that 'one half of the townspeople are Non-conformist'.

A wave of building followed, beginning with a new Primitive Methodist chapel in Old Street in 1870. Zion Methodists built a chapel on New Road in 1881, but the most remarkable achievement was that of the Wesleyans. Desiring a better building than their chapel in Lower Broad Street, they purchased land in Old Street and Broad Street. 'With a maximum of faith, but a minimum of cash' they built a new chapel in Broad Street in 1879, with seating for 700 people, turned their former premises into a school, and used the Old Street property as a manse. With a loan of £4,000 to repay, it seemed they had over-reached themselves, but the situation was turned around during the inspirational ministry of Revd. Thomas Riley from 1892. He promoted 'self-denial weeks', raised the Broad Street membership to 447 - and saw all debts paid within three years!

A seminal moment for Methodism came in 1898 when one of their number, Gaius Smith, grocer, became Mayor, and took the Council, with the maces, to morning service in Broad Street, rather than to St Laurence's. In partisan, sectarian Ludlow this was a bold move - and many saw it, and long remembered it, as proof that Non-Conformity had come of age in Ludlow.

Health, education and pleasure

Ludlow had eight doctors and a dentist in 1888, most of them in Broad Street, but the poor depended heavily on charity, especially on the Public Dispensary, supported by voluntary contributions. This had been refounded in 1835 and treated some 300 patients a year. One of Ludlow's most characteristic Victorian institutions was the Cottage Hospital, established in 1874 'for the relief of the labouring classes'.

The Cottage Hospital in College Street, photographed before its closure in 1982. It was converted from a private house, which had been created from the Palmers' Guild College. Endowments included £3,000 from the Hon. Mary Windsor-Clive.

By 1901 the National Schools in Galdeford and East Hamlet and the British School (opened 1898) in Old Street provided elementary places for all children, though many attended the town's private schools. The Grammar School thrived intermittently, especially during the Headmastership of Dr. Sparrow (1865-86), but there was no secondary education for girls. A Mechanics Institute for working men had been opened in 1840.

Leisure habits changed considerably. Many traditional pastimes declined, including Maypole Dancing (still practised in Holdgate Fee in 1870), the Shrove Tuesday Tug-of-War, and the public bonfires on 5 November. Merry-making ceased to accompany most of the fairs but the May Fair became largely a pleasure fair, with 'thousands from the surrounding districts' resorting in 1844 to 'Wombwell's menagerie, minor shows and exhibiting amusements'. Team games became popular, with records of cricket and football at Ludford Park in the 1850s, and clubs were formed later for bowls, tennis, golf and hockey. Dramatic productions and concerts became popular, Ludlow's oldest society being the Choral Society, founded in 1858. Public spectacles drew large crowds, among them the parades of the Volunteers, wearing spiked helmets and accompanied by the Town Band.

CHAPTER NINE

THE TWENTIETH CENTURY

Local government

Shropshire County Council was formed in 1889 and Ludlow had one of the 51 seats. It took over education, roads and other services during the early years. Ludlow Borough Council retained most of its Victorian responsibilities, but by the 1920s was also providing municipal housing. There were four wards - Broad Street, Corve Street, East Hamlet and Old Street - each of which had an Alderman and three councillors.

The difficulties faced by many small councils caused a major restructuring of local government in 1967. Amidst great local regret, Ludlow was one of the towns which lost its borough status, and many of its functions were transferred to Ludlow Rural District Council which had offices at Stone House in Corve Street. There were further changes in 1974, when South Shropshire District Council was formed. Ludlow became a Town Council of parish council status, though it retained its Mayor and ownership of the Guildhall and Butter Cross. Many thought this a sad end to centuries of civic independence. During these years the social range of Borough Councillors was wider than previously, though there were still tradesmen such as W.J. Brown, chemist, S. Price, baker, and J. Davies, newsagent. The Council's officers during these years included W.C. Tyrell from 1918 to 1946, who claimed to be the only Town Clerk in England with the initials of a public lavatory!

The last meeting of Ludlow Borough Council in 1967. The splendid Council Chamber is packed with guests. The Mayor, Councillor Bill Price, plumber, is in the chair, flanked by Councillor Ted Sheldon on his right and the Town Clerk, J.Mallony, on his left. The speaker, on her feet, is Alderman Gladys Potter, who was made a Freeman of the Borough for her services to the town.

The Expanding Town

The combined population of Ludlow and East Hamlet dropped slightly between 1901 and 1931, but had recovered to 6,530 by 1951. Between that year and 1991 there was a striking rise of 30% to reach 9,011 in 1991, while 9,320 was estimated for 1996. As shown on Fig. 24, the town's physical area also expanded, the built up area in 1999 being about three times that of 1901. The by-pass, opened in 1977, provided a clear boundary to the north-east, but by 1999 most of the land between it and the historic town had been built up, or designated as a preserved open space.

Ludlow sustained its role as a market and service centre throughout this period. A study of 21 service and retailing centres on the central Welsh border in 1964 showed that Ludlow was first of five second rank centres, the others being Leominster, Welshpool, Newtown and Llandrindod Wells. They were well behind Shrewsbury and Hereford, but ahead of smaller towns such as Knighton and Hay-on-Wye. Some of the post-1951 expansion was due to the increasing importance of manufacturing, which employed 22% of workers in the 1980s. Some factory workers came into Ludlow each day, but these were offset by Ludlow people who travelled to work elsewhere, e.g. on buses to work at a poultry-processing plant at Craven Arms.

Ludlow's rural setting and historic heritage have been the basis of its tourist trade, which has been a factor in the town's economy throughout the twentieth century. This too has promoted employment, especially in catering and in tourist orientated shops. By 1999, remarkably, the town had three Michelin-starred restaurants, more than anywhere outside London - and was called 'the gastronomic capital of the countryside'.

Another reason for the town's growth was its attractiveness for retirement, so that by the 1980s 24% of residents were of retirement age. This was higher than the figure for Shropshire, which was 18%, but considerably less than the 39% at Church Stretton, the county's most specialised retirement town. Ludlow's reputation as a pleasant place in which to live grew in the 1990s. An article in Country Life in April 1999 described Ludlow as 'the most vibrant small town in the country' and claimed that it had become 'a paradigm for a modern kind of civilised living'. The fact that Ludlow is an hour's drive from a motorway, often a matter for regret, was seen as an inducement by some people.

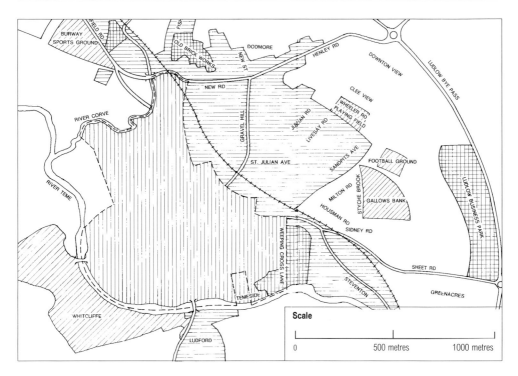

FIG. 24 Ludlow in the 1990s, based on Proposals Map No.52, South Shropshire Local Plan, 1992

This diagramatic map is adapted from proposals Map No.52 of the South Shropshire Local Plan, 1992. It shows the historic town lying east and north of the River Teme, with Whitcliffe Common and the ancient core of Ludford to the south-west. To the north east and north are the areas mostly covered with suburbs by 1939, with a number of roads named. The railway, running diagonally across the map, divides much of this suburban growth from the historic town. The area of post-World War Two expansion, now reaching as far as the by-pass, is left unshaded but some housing estates and the main recreational areas are marked, as is Ludlow Business Park, formerly the Sheet Road Industrial Estate. Other features marked include the old brick works off New Road, and the industrial areas on Bromfield Road and Weeping Cross Lane. Although many people now live in the suburbs, shops and services are heavily concentrated in the historic town.

Key

_ _ _ borough boundary pre-1832

historic town

open space

area developed by 1939

industrial

++++++++ railway

149

Housing

Large houses continued to be built in Ludlow's eastern suburbs, especially in St Julian's Avenue, where plots were available for purchase from 1902. Some houses were constructed by Turford and Southward, whose yard was in Upper Galdeford (later Bufton's). In contrast, a number of cottages in backyards were condemned in 1913 as unfit for habitation. With the aid of Government subsidy the first Council houses in Ludlow were built at Temeside in the 1920s, part of the nation-wide 'Homes Fit for Heroes' campaign. There were later estates at Henley Road, Sandpits Avenue and Steventon, bringing the number of houses to 88 by 1931, though some of these were of low quality and lacked indoor toilets. Poor housing conditions in parts of Ludlow were exposed by The Ludlow Advertiser in 1931. The Reader of St Laurence's, Revd. R.G. Channer, offended many when he spoke from the pulpit of Ludlow's hovels:

> 'How could Ludlow residents sit and listen to the church bells playing Home, Sweet Home, while they knew that a hundred yards away people lived in hovels where pools of water poured in through the roofs'.

The provision of council housing continued after the war, beginning with prefabricated bungalows and Airey houses at Clee View, and the former also on Temeside. Later there were large estates at Dodmore and Hucklemarsh, and above Styche Brook. Private housing estates were built further out, as at Greenacres, Bringewood and Stanton Road.

We can journey from this spot to one in the opposite direction, I mean Lower Galdeford. Here we find another house where there are six children and a man and wife. For over two years the roof has leaked every time it rains, necessitating the people getting out of bed to move it to a dry spot at another end of the room. "Does the landlord know?" And the reply is: "I'm tired of telling him."

While talking to this person I was asked into the living room, which, owing to the damp on the walls, was devoid of wallpaper, and I asked where the stairs were by which one went to the bedrooms. I was led to what was called the back kitchen, and there were the stairs. But the back kitchen walls were unplastered, the floor had no cement or tiles, simply the earth visible. The stairs were nothing but steps that a farmer would use to go from a stable to a hay loft.

From ***The Ludlow Advertiser,*** 24 Jan. 1931, part of a series of reports and letters on housing.

Part of Ludlow's first Council estate, built in Temeside and Holdgate Fee in the late 1920s. These are better houses than some built later.

Part of Ballard's Close and Vashon Close, built on the far east of the town in the late 1990s. Both are named after admirals born in Ludlow.

The market in 1916, looking towards Station Drive and Corve Street.

The shop of Charles Griffiths, butcher, at 26 Bull Ring, c.1905.

Pepper Lane Antiques in 1999, occupying a 12th century burgage.

DMS Plastics on Ludlow Business Park, opened 1996; 55 are employed.

Employment

The livestock market remained the lifeblood of the town. There were two firms with adjoining yards in Corve Street which amalgamated as Morris, Barker and Poole by 1934, later becoming part of McCartneys. Country folk poured in on Mondays, Julian Critchley writing in The London Illustrated News in 1972 describes Ludlow as a 'workaday town with farmers' wives in Doris Archer hats.' Movement of the livestock market to Ox Pasture on Overton Road in 1994 enabled expansion and Ludlow is now second to Carlisle for selling fat cattle.

Family retail businesses predominated at first, the largest in the 1920s being J. Evans and Son, drapers, at 1, 2, 4 and 5 King Street. Multiple firms appeared, Boots taking over Woodhouse and Son, chemists, by 1937. In 1967 Ludlow had 11 butchers and 13 grocers, but numbers were reduced by the 1990s, when the town had two supermarkets: a reflection of a nationwide trend. A growth area was in antiques, with the number of businesses increasing from three in 1967 to more than 12 in the 1990s. The town also had a number of craft shops, art galleries and second-hand bookshops.

There were small factory industries before 1939, such as Temeside Casemills, making boxes for jewellery. In 1946 a foodstore in Weeping Cross Lane was acquired by McConnells, Ltd, makers of hedge cutters and agricultural machinery. E.J. Walters and Co, clothing manufacturers, who began in 1957 in a redundant chapel with a sewing machine, became Ludlow's largest employer by the 1970s, but later moved most of their plant elsewhere. Another major employer is Lloyds of Ludlow Ltd, International Contractors and Hauliers, a huge concern growing from a small business over half a century. In the late 1990s there were a range of light industries, many of them at Ludlow Business Park on Sheet Road.

Traffic and Parking

The reconciliation of motor traffic with narrow streets and ancient buildings has been a major concern for many historic towns. The traffic along Corve Street and Old Street, part of the A49, increased after 1918, so that in 1931 the road later known as Coronation Avenue was opened to reduce congestion in lower Corve Street. Away from the through route, however, photographs reveal half-empty streets on most days of the week.

As traffic problems increased after 1945, concern for the town centre grew, causing Nikolaus Pevsner to write in 1958: 'may Ludlow never decide to pull down its tortuous centre to please the gentleman motorist or the charabanc tourist.' Partly due to lack of potential investors, Ludlow was spared the insensitive developments which afflicted many towns in the 1960s, but parking became a serious problem. A proposal by the County Council in 1959 to widen Broad Street by removing the cobbles provoked fervent opposition, led by the Rector, Bishop Sara. The cobbles remained in place, but later objections to Castle Street car-park were unheeded. More parking was later provided by S.S.D.C in Upper and Lower Galdeford. The most important measure was the Ludlow by-pass, opened in 1977 after long debate about its route. Tower Street was pedestrianised in 1989 and in the 1990s plans were being made for limited enhancement of the town centre.

This still from a cine-film of Ludlow made in 1930 catches the unhurried atmosphere of the town. To some degree this reflects the economic difficulties of the time - Ludlow did not totally escape the blight of unemployment. There are also hints of the small town idyll which attracted, such artists as Winifred Knights and Leslie Ward.

Conservation

The cult of antiquarianism, especially towards timber-framed buildings, is rooted in the nineteenth century, but it became fashionable after 1900. The premises of F.J. Bodenham and No. 45 Bull Ring were stripped of plaster in 1913, and the process continued after 1918, as at the top of Broad Street. Conservation became a national movement, with the introduction of statutory powers in 1947. Ludlow Civic Society was formed in 1954 and promoted many projects, one of them at the Tolsey. In 1970 the historic core of Ludlow became a conservation area, with 469 listed buildings - a higher proportion to population than at any other town except Bradford-on-Avon. The number was increased to 502 in 1992, and the conservation area extended to include Whitcliffe and parts of Lower Galdeford and Steventon.

The replacement of glazing bars at 8 Corve Street is one of many improvements which collectively have enhanced Ludlow. Caring owners, an enlightened Conservation Officer and an active Civic Society can share the credit.

The conservation record is mixed, with many fine schemes by private individuals and public bodies offset by some disasters. The most controversial was the demolition of the Town Hall by S.S.D.C. in 1986, nineteen years after taking over the building from the Borough Council. This was welcomed by those who disliked the building - Pevsner called it 'Ludlow's bad luck' - but others lamented the loss of a valued public amenity. A less obvious loss was the truncation or over-building of many historic burgage plots for car-parks or new housing developments, especially on the north side of Upper Galdeford and west of Holdgate Fee.

There have been other conservation groups and projects, beginning with the Whitcliffe Commoners, re-activated in 1923, later the Friends of Whitcliffe Common. A huge restoration project at St Laurence's in the 1950s was preceded by the formation of the Friends of St Laurence in 1943 and followed by the Fabric Trust for St Laurence in 1996. The Weirs Trust, to restore the town's historic weirs, was formed in 1997.

Welfare and amenities

Some Ludlovians lived in comfort before 1939 but others did not. There were great improvements as insanitary courts were cleared. Medical care became more readily available after 1948, Broad Street remaining Ludlow's Harley Street until the 1980s, when two purpose-built centres were built in Upper Galdeford. For most people, living standards rose sharply, and by 1991 nearly seven out of ten Ludlow households had at least one car. There were changes in the education system, from the foundation of Ludlow Girls High School in 1910 to the opening of Ludlow Sixth Form College in 1977, with Ludlow School a feeder comprehensive school. Over two thirds of school leavers went to further education in the 1990s.

Amenities before 1939 included two picture houses, a drill hall, a roller-skating rink and a number of playing fields. The Town Hall was much used for drama and dances. A swimming pool at Dinham, financed by community effort, opened in 1961. In the 1970s the National School became the Bishop Mascall diocesan centre. Closure of the cinemas and demolition of the Town Hall left Ludlow short of facilities after 1986; but inititiatives by the councils and local groups provided a fine Community and Arts Centre at the Assembly Rooms, a spacious Leisure Centre and Swimming Pool at Ludlow School, and the Rockspring Community Centre in the Sandpits Area. A town museum re-opened over the Butter Cross in 1955, with John Norton, later M.B.E., as its dedicated curator. It was praised by Ian Nairn in 1972 as 'the best local museum I've seen in Britain.' A museum display of Ludlow's history is now at the Assembly Rooms, while a new library and museum centre are planned for soon after 2,000.

Dinham Swimming Pool, which used the old Castle Mill premises as changing rooms. The cruck-like timber supports were a feature of the building.

The Rockspring Community Centre near Rock Lane, incorporating the Baptist Chapel. It is a valued community focus.

A centre for tourists and the arts

Motor transport quickened Ludlow's development as a tourist centre. There was a spate of travel books, such as S.R. Jones's *Touring England by Road and Byway* in 1927, which pronounced that 'Ludlow, with its bold hillside situation, its inns and its quaint byways, is a wonderful place'. Tourism became more professional towards the end of the century, and by the 1990s there was a Tourist Information Centre.

Ludlow is a centre for the arts. The town has high quality societies for art, music, drama and photography, and the late 1990s have seen concerts in the parish church by the conductor Sir Simon Rattle and the pianist Vladimir Ashkenazy. The major event is now The Ludlow Festival, the roots of which go back to 1934, when a spectacular Shropshire Pageant was staged in Ludlow Castle, with a tercentary anniversary performance of Comus. There were further productions of Comus in 1953, 1958 and 1959 as part of an ambitious fund-raising programme for the restoration of St Laurence's, with other plays in intervening years. Their success led to an annual Ludlow Festival from 1960. This has become one of the country's leading arts festivals, with open air Shakespeare in the castle as its centre-piece. The inner bailey provides a superb auditorium, a *Financial Times* reviewer writing of Othello in 1974 that: 'Voices bounce off the rugged walls ... like balls from a squash court'

Reviewers catch the special atmosphere of the Ludlow Festival. 'The whole town is en fete', wrote one in 1980. Blankets and flasks carried by evening play-goers were seen as a symbol of Ludlow, 'akin to Wimbledon's strawberry teas'. 21 plays have been presented, with four productions of A Midsummer Night's Dream, and three of Macbeth, Twelfth Night, Hamlet and Richard III. Good team performances are the strength of Ludlow Festival, but there have been big names such as Edward Woodward, whose Richard III in 1982 was rated 'the best since Olivier'. There are more than 20 supporting events a year, including recitals in the church and pop concerts in the outer bailey. The 1999 Festival ended magnificently with a rock concert by The Royal Family and the Counterfeit Stones, culminating in fireworks.

A scene from the 1969 production of Romeo and Juliet, Angela Pleasance as Juliet and Philip Lowrie as Romeo.

Bonds, loyalties and divisions

There were many close-knit kinship networks in Ludlow, especially among the lower income groups. Householders in 1938 included 33 Prices, 27 Lewis's, 24 Edwards's and 21 Griffiths's, with 12 Adams's, 11 Lellos, and eight Bradleys, Bromleys and Nash's. A Ludlovian born in the 1940s recalls that 'in general people cared for each other'. In his street 'if someone died then every curtain used to be drawn as a sign of respect'.

At all social levels there were groups – centred round a church, a society or a pub – to attract people's loyalties. By the 1960s there were ten churches in the town, including St. Peter's, a Roman Catholic church built in the Byzantine style in 1936. Societies and clubs multiplied, with many uniformed organisations including branches of the Red Cross and St John's Ambulance. For many, pubs like The Hen and Chickens, 'a singing pub', were focal points, with leagues for darts and dominoes. Another popular sport was pigeon fancying, with cages peppering Dodmore, Sandpits and elsewhere.

Though these allegiances frequently overlapped, Ludlow society as a whole was often deeply divided. Before 1939 the range of wealth and living standards was enormous, often within single streets. Aristocratic hauteur was often apparent, as in the 1920s when, a grocer later recalled: 'Most county ladies did not go into the shops. They sounded their car horns and an assistant ran out and took down the order.' Later, there was often tension between native Ludlovians and 'newcomers.'

In the last decades of the century Ludlow has been beset by planning issues, though the deep animosity of the 1840s has been avoided. The route of the by-pass – east of the town on farmland or through Whitcliffe by a cutting - aroused great passion in the 1960s and 1970s. In the 1980s and 1990s there have been planning inquiries about the building of a sports hall at Ludlow College, about the provision of another supermarket and about proposals made in draft local plans. As this book goes to press there is debate about a proposal to locate a new football ground and facilities on Overton Road. Such disputes reflect different perceptions about the sort of place Ludlow should be: some are concerned to preserve it as a small town of beauty and charm, others give priority to employment and facilities for education and leisure.

War and Peace

The first years of the century saw British Imperialism at its most rampant. Ludlovians sang Rule Britannia with gusto at the end of Town Hall concerts and patriotic crowds cheered the first volunteers as they marched to Ludlow station in 1914. The World

Wars took a heavy toll of Ludlovians, as they did of people from every town: 137 were killed in 1914-18 and 38 in 1939-45, with two more dying in Korea. The town applauded heroes, as in September 1940, when 'hundreds lined the streets' for the funeral of Pilot Officer Whitbread, killed in the Battle of Britain.

The desire to avoid such conflicts was a reason for the twinning movement after 1945. In 1988 Ludlow was paired with La Ferté Macé, a historic French town in south Normandy near Lassy, where the Lacys came from in 1066. In 1994 there was a twin-

The Ludlow Town Hall plaster cast. The Boer War memorial itself still stands proudly in Adelaide.

ning with San Pietro in Cariano, in Italy near Verona. Another European link has been established between St. Laurence's and a church in Nuremberg.

The changing attitude to war is illustrated by the memorials shown. The memorial, above, once in Ludlow Town Hall, is a plaster cast of the Boer War memo-

rial in Adelaide, Australia, by Captain Adrian Jones (1845-1938), son of a Ludlow veterinary surgeon. It shows a mounted cavalry man, grasping his rifle and poised for battle. The memorial, left, by Walenty Pytewl of Ross-on-Wye, an extra-patriate Pole, is quite different. Commissioned by the Ludlow Branch of the Royal British Legion in 1998, it shows doves, symbols of peace, surmounting the Christian cross of suffering and reconciliation. To be set in Ludlow, at the heart of the Welsh Marches, at the end of a millennium of conflict, it looks forward in hope to a millennium of peace - there is no better way to end this history.

A model of the intended Ludlow memorial, which will stand in front of 14 Castle Street. It was decided after 1918 to commemorate the Ludlow dead by inscribed plaques in the south porch of the parish church, but there is now a wish for a memorial in one of the town's main streets.

Select Bibliography

A. MANUSCRIPT SOURCES
Bodleian Library, Oxford
MS Ashmole 854: ff.178-186
British Library
Liber Landavensis (Cotton Nero A IV) [transcribed by M.A.Faraday]
Herefordshire Record Office
Probate records; diocesan records (HD); Acts of Office [transcribed by M.A. Faraday]
National Library of Wales
Powis Castle papers
Public Record Office
Various collections, including Chancery (C.), Exchequer. (E.), King's Bench (KB 26/27), Probate (Prob.11) [MAF];
Taxation (T47), Census returns (HO)
Shropshire County Museum (Ludlow)
Griffiths' Scrapbook, 1816-26
Shropshire Records and Research Centre, Shrewsbury
Ludlow Borough Archives [transcribed by M.A. Faraday, the author and others];

LB 1:   incorporation
LB 2:   Borough Corporation Minutes (8 volumes)
LB 3:   Appointment of burgesses and officers
LB 4:   Estates: 1, title deeds; 2, rentals and renters' accounts; 3, leases; 4, surveys; 5, tolls; 6, mills; 7, timber; 8, transfer of Palmers' Guild land; 9, weights; 10, fisheries
LB 5:   Palmers' Guild
LB 6:   Manorial
LB 7:   Administration
LB 8:   Financial
LB 9:   Borough Court
LB 10: Court Leet and View of Frankpledge
LB 11: Quarter Sessions
LB 12: Coroner
LB 13: Assize
LB 14: Council of the Marches in Wales
LB 15: Parish Records
LB 16: Guild of Hammermen
LB 17: Guild of Stitchmen
LB 18: Ludlow Turnpike Trusts
LB 19: Police
LB 20: Ludlow Association for the Persecution of Felons
LB 21: Ludlow Natural History Society

Deposited collections, including Clark (1141), Ludford Park (11), Mead (1623, 2705), Morgan (786, 5411), Salwey and Rickards (2030)

B. PRINTED COLLECTIONS OF DOCUMENTS

Registers of the Bishops of Hereford, Canterbury and York Society, 1906-1919
Calendars of State Papers Domestic
Calendar of Patent Rolls
Parliamentary Papers

C. NEWSPAPERS

Gloucester Journal (from 1722), Hereford Journal (from 1770), Ludlow Advertiser (from 1888), Ludlow Postman (1719-20), Salopian Journal (from 1794), Shrewsbury Chronicle (from 1772), Worcester Journal (from 1712)

D. TRADE DIRECTORIES

Universal British, 1794; Holden, 1814, 1817; Pigot, 1822, 1828, 1835; Robson, 1840; Pigot, 1842, 1844; Slater 1849, 1850; Bagshaw, 1851; Kelly, 1856; Cassey, 1858; Kelly, 1863; Slater, 1868; Kelly, 1870; Casey, 1871, 1875; Mercer and Crocker, 1877; Slater, 1879; Kelly, 1879, 1885; Parker, 1888; Kelly, 1890, 1895, 1900, 1905, 1909, 1913; Bennet, 1916; Kelly, 1917, 1922, 1929, 1936, 1941; 1967

E. MAPS

Wood, J., Plan of Ludlow, 1835 (copy in Ludlow Museum)
O.S. 1:500 (1885)

F. PRINTED SOURCES AND UNPUBLISHED THESES

Abbreviation: T.S.A.S. Transactions of the Shropshire Archaeological Society
Bateson, M., 'The Laws of Breteuil', English Historical Review, 15, 1900, pp.73, 302, 496, 754.
Borsay, P., The English Urban Renaissance: Culture and Society in the Provincial Town, 1660-1770, Oxford, 1989
Clive, R.H., Documents connected with the History of Ludlow, Ludlow, 1841
Colvin, H.M.(Ed.), The History of the King's Works, Vols.II & III, H.M.S.O., 1963
Conzen, M.R.G., 'The use of town plans in the study of Urban History', in Dyos, H.J. (Ed,), The Study of Urban History, London 1968, pp.124-26.
Cranage, D.H.S., An Architectural Account of the Churches of Shropshire, part 2, The Hundred of Munslow, 1895, pp.105-142.
Dineley, T., The Account of the Official Progress of his Grace Henry the first Duke of Beaufort, 1684; facsimile 1888.
Dodd, A.H., Studies in Stuart Wales, Cardiff, 1971, pp.49-75.
Earp, J.R. and Hains, B.A., The Welsh Borderland, British Regional Geology, 3rd Ed., London, 1971
Elliot, E., A History of Congregationalism in Shropshire, Oswestry, 1898
Faraday, M.A., 'The Ludlow Poll Tax Returns of 1667', T.S.A.S., LIX,1971-72, pp.104-123.
Faraday, M.A., Ludlow 1085-1660: A Social, Economic and Political History, Chichester, 1991
Fay, A.M., Victorian Days in England, Boston, U.S.A., 1923.
Felton, W., A Description of the Town of Ludlow, Ludlow, 1811
Felton, W., Copies of the Charters and Grants to the town of Ludlow, Ludlow, 1821
Ganderton, E.W. and Larford, J, Ludlow Stained and Painted Glass, 1961.
Hathaway, E.J. Ricketts, P.T. Robson, C.A. and Wiltshire, A.D., Fouke Fitz Waryn. Anglo-Norman texts, 1975

Hussey, C., 'Ludlow', Country Life, 21 Dec, 28 Dec, 1945. 8 Feb, 15 Feb, 1946 Munslow, 1895, pp.105-142.

Klein, P., The Misericords of Ludlow Parish Church, Ludlow, 1986

Klein, P. and Roe, A., The Carmelite Friary, Corve Street, Ludlow: Its History and Excavation

Lloyd, D.J. 'Popular Education and Society in Ludlow, 1711-1861', unpublished M.Ed. thesis, Hull, 1974

Lloyd, D.J. and Moran, M., The Corner Shop, Ludlow Research Paper No. 2, 1978

Lloyd, D.J., Broad Street, Ludlow Research Paper No.3, 1979

Lloyd, D.J. and Klein, P., Ludlow: A Historic Town in Words and Pictures, Chichester, 1984

Lloyd, D.J., King, R., Sykes, M., Ludlow Festival: the first Twenty Five Years,1984

Lloyd, D.J., Howell, P. and Richards, M., The Feathers, Ludlow Research Paper No.6,1980

Ludlow Heritage News, various issues from May 1984

Ludlow Parish Registers, Shropshire Parish Registers, Diocese of Hereford series, XII, XIII(1913)

Macky, J., A Journey through England, Vol.II, 1722

Ogilby, J., Britannia London, 1675

Oman, C., Ayot Rectory, London, 1965.

Pevsner, N., Shropshire, Buildings of England series, 1958

St. John Hope, W.H., 'The Ancient Topography of the Town of Ludlow', Archaeologia, LXI, 1909, p.383-388

St. John Hope, W.H., 'The Castle of Ludlow', Archaeologia, LXI, 1909, pp.257-358

Sargent, M., My Old Man the Gasman, Excellent Press, Ludlow, 1998

Shepherd, F.G., The Parish Church of Ludlow, Ludlow, 1944

Skeel, C.A.J., The Council in the Marches of Wales, London, 1904

Smith, W.J., Herbert Correspondence, Cardiff, 1968

Somerset, J.A.B., Records of Early English Drama: Shropshire, I, The Records; II, Editorial Apparatus, Toronto, 1994

South Shropshire District Council, Ludlow District Plan, 1978

South Shropshire District Council, South Shropshire Local Plan, 1992

Sparrow, Rev. W.C., 'The Palmers Guild of Ludlow', T.S.A.S., 1, 1878, pp.333-394

Speight, M. and Lloyd, D.J., Ludlow Houses and their Residents, Ludlow Research Paper No.1,1977

Speight, M., The Great House: Number 112, Corve Street, Ludlow, 1270-1980, Ludlow Research Paper No. 4,1980

Speight, M., St Giles' Church,Ludford: A History and Guide, Ludford, nd

Trinder, B., A History of Shropshire, Chichester,1983

Trinder, B., The Industrial Archaeology of Shropshire, Chichester, 1996

Victoria County History of Shropshire, Vol.I (1909), II (1973), III (1979), IV (1989)

Watkins-Pritchard, W. (Ed.), The Shropshire Hearth Tax of 1672, Shrewsbury, 1949

Weyman, H.T., 'The Members of Parliament for Ludlow', T.S.A.S., ser. 2,VII, 1895, pp.1-54

Weyman, H.T., Ludlow in Bye-Gone Days, Ludlow, 1913

Whiteman, A. (Ed.), The Compton Census of 1676, Oxford,1986

Wightman, W.E., The Lacy Family in England and Normandy, 1066-1194, Oxford, 1966

Williams, P., 'Government and Politics in Ludlow, 1590-1642', T.S.A.S. 56 (1957), pp.282-94.

Williams, P., The Council in the Marches of Wales under Elizabeth the First, Cardiff, 1958

Wright, S., 'Sojourners and Lodgers in a Provincial Town: the evidence of 18th century Ludlow', Urban History Yearbook, XVIII, 1990, pp.14-35

Wright, S., 'Holding up half the sky: women and their occupations in eighteenth century Ludlow', Midland History, XIV, pp..53-74.

Wright, T. senior, The History and Antiquities of the Town of Ludlow, Ludlow, 1826

Wright, T., History of Ludlow, 1852

Wright, T., Churchwardens' Accounts of the Town of Ludlow, 1540-74, Camden Society, 1869

INDEX